HERITAGE AUCTIONS HA.com BID SHEET

3500 Maple Avenue | Dallas, Texas 75219-3941
Direct Client Service Line – Toll Free: 866-835-3243 | Fax: 214-409-1425

ALL INFORMATION MUST BE COMPLETED AND FORM SIGNED

Auction #5149

CLIENT# (IF KNOWN)

❑ Mr. ❑ Mrs. ❑ Ms. ❑ Dr.
NAME

ADDRESS

CITY **STATE** **ZIP CODE** **COUNTRY**

EMAIL

(COUNTRY CODE) **DAY PHONE**   (COUNTRY CODE) **NIGHT PHONE**

(COUNTRY CODE) **CELL**   (COUNTRY CODE) **FAX**

❑ IF NECESSARY, PLEASE INCREASE MY BIDS BY ❑1 ❑2 ❑3 INCREMENT(S)
Lots will be purchased as much below top bids as possible.

❑ I WANT TO LIMIT MY BIDDING TO A TOTAL OF $ _____
at the hammer amount for all lots listed on this bid sheet. I am aware that by utilizing the Budget Bidding feature, all bids on this sheet will be affected. If I intend to have regular bidding on other lots I will need to use a separate bid sheet.

Do you want to receive an email, text message, or fax confirming receipt of your bids?
❑ Email   ❑ Cell Phone Text   ❑ Fax

Payment by check may result in your property not being released until purchase funds clear our bank. Checks must be drawn on a U.S. bank. All bids are subject to the applicable Buyer's Premium. See HA.com for details.

I have read and agree to all of the Terms and Conditions of Auction: inclusive of paying interest at the lesser of 1.5% per month (18% per annum) or the maximum contract interest rate under applicable state law from the date of auction.

REFERENCES: New bidders who are unknown to us must furnish satisfactory industry references or a valid credit card in advance of the auction date.

(Signature required) *Please make a copy of this bid sheet for your records.*

❑ I HAVE PREVIOUSLY BOUGHT FROM HERITAGE AUCTIONS

❑ I HAVE A RESALE PERMIT – *please contact 800-872-6467*

Non-Internet bids (including but not limited to, podium, fax, phone and mail bids) may be submitted at any time and are treated similar to floor bids. These types of bids must be on-increment or at a half increment (called a cut bid). Any podium, fax, phone or mail bids that do not conform to a full or half increment will be rounded up or down to the nearest full or half increment and will be considered your high bid.

Current Bid	Bid Increment
< – $10	$1
$10 – $29	$2
$30 – $49	$3
$50 – $99	$5
$100 – $199	$10
$200 – $299	$20
$300 – $499	$25
$500 – $999	$50
$1,000 – $1,999	$100
$2,000 – $2,999	$200
$3,000 – $4,999	$250
$5,000 – $9,999	$500
$10,000 – $19,999	$1,000
$20,000 – $29,999	$2,000
$30,000 – $49,999	$2,500
$50,000 – $99,999	$5,000
$100,000 – $199,999	$10,000
$200,000 – $299,999	$20,000
$300,000 – $499,999	$25,000
$500,000 – $999,999	$50,000
$1,000,000 – $1,999,999	$100,000
$2,000,000 – $2,999,999	$200,000
$3,000,000 – $4,999,999	$250,000
$5,000,000 – $9,999,999	$500,000
>$10,000,000	$1,000,000

Bid in whole dollar amounts only.   **Please print your bids.**

LOT NO.	AMOUNT	LOT NO.	AMOUNT	LOT NO.	AMOUNT

REV. 7-30-13

Last Name: _____

Bid in whole dollar amounts only.   Please print your bids.

LOT NO.	AMOUNT	LOT NO.	AMOUNT	LOT NO.	AMOUNT

Please make a copy of this bid sheet for your records.

7 Easy Ways to Bid

1. Internet
Simply go to www.HA.com, find the auction you are looking for and click "View Lots" or type your desired Lot # into the "Search" field. Every lot is listed with full descriptions and images. Enter your bid and click "Place Bid." Internet bids will be accepted until 10:00 PM CT the day before the live auction session takes place.

2. e-Mail
You can also e-mail your bids to us at Bid@HA.com. List lot numbers and bids, and include your name, address, phone, and customer # (if known) as well as a statement of your acceptance of the Terms and Conditions of Sale. Email bids will be accepted up to 24 hours before the live auction.

3. Postal Mail
Simply complete the Bid Sheet on the reverse side of this page with your bids on the lots you want, sign it and mail it in. If yours is the high bid on any lot, we act as your representative at the auction and buy the lot as cheaply as competition permits.

4. In Person
Come to the auction and view the lots in person and bid live on the floor.

5. FAX
Follow the instructions for completing your mail bid, but this time FAX it to (214) 409-1425. FAX bids will be accepted until 12:00 p.m. CT the day prior to the auction date.

6. Live By Phone
Call 1-800-872-6467 Ext. 1150 and ask for phone bidding assistance at least 24 hours prior to the auction.

7. Live using HERITAGE Live!®
Auctions designated as "Heritage Live Enabled" have continuous bidding from the time the auction is posted on our site through the live event. When normal Internet bidding ends, visit HA.com/Live and continue to place Live Proxy bids. When the item hits the auction block, you can continue to bid live against the floor and other live bidders.

Because of the many avenues by which bids may be submitted, there is the real possibility of a tie for the high bid. In the event of a tie, Internet bidders, within their credit limit, will win by default.

Heritage Signature® Auction #5149 & 5158

American Paintings, Drawings & Sculpture & The Art of New York

December 5, 2013 | New York

Signature® Floor Sessions 1-2
(Floor, Telephone, HERITAGE Live!,® Internet, Fax, and Mail)

2 E. 79th Street • New York, NY 10075
(Ukrainian Institute of American at The Fletcher-Sinclair Mansion)

Session 1 - THE ART OF NEW YORK #5158
Thursday, December 5 • 2:00 PM ET • Lots 65001–65047

Session 2 - AMERICAN PAINTINGS, DRAWINGS & SCULPTURE #5149
Thursday, December 5 • 3:00 PM ET • Lots 64001-64187

LOT SETTLEMENT AND PICK-UP
Sessions 1 & 2 lots will be available for pick-up at the Ukrainian Institute of America at the Fletcher-Sinclair Mansion during or immediately following each session on December 5. If you wish for your purchases to remain in our NY office for pickup after the auction, please make arrangements with either Abel Privado at 214-409-1379 / AbelP@HA.com or Cassandra Hutzler at 212-486-3517/CassandraH@ HA.com by 12:00 PM ET on Thursday, December 5. Otherwise the property will be transported back to Dallas. Any lots left in NY can be picked up at our NY office beginning 1 PM on Monday, December 9 by appointment only. Any lots not picked up at the Ukrainian Institute of America at the Fletcher-Sinclair Mansion will be available for pick-up at the Heritage Design District Annex, 1518 Slocum St., Dallas, TX 75207, after Tuesday, December 10, by appointment only. See back of this catalog for information to arrange third party shipping arrangements of your purchases.

Please note: Lot #64100 is located in Bridgeport, Connecticut. To make an appointment to view the piece, please contact Aviva Lehmann at avival@ha.com in our New York office. Buyer will be responsible for de-installation and transport from its current location.

Lots are sold at an approximate rate of 60 lots per hour, but it is not uncommon to sell 50 lots or 100 lots in any given hour.

Buyer's Premium: 25% on the first $100,000 (minimum $14), 20% of any amount between $100,000 and $1,000,000, and 12% of any amount over $1,000,000.

NYC Auctioneer licenses: Samuel Foose 0952360; Robert Korver 1096338; Kathleen Guzman 0762165; Michael J. Sadler 1304630; Scott Peterson 1306933; Andrea Voss 1320558; Nicholas Dawes 1304724; Ed Beardsley 1183220; Clinton Swett 1407750. New York City #41513036 and NYC Second Hand Dealers License #1364739]

This Auction is presented and cataloged by Heritage Auctions

© 2013 Heritage Auctioneers & Galleries, Inc.

HERITAGE is a registered trademark and service mark of Heritage Capital Corporation. Registered in U.S. Patent and Trademark Office.

LOT VIEWING
2 E. 79th Street • New York, NY 10075
(Ukrainian Institute of American at The Fletcher-Sinclair Mansion)

Tuesday, December 3 • 10:00 AM – 9:00 PM ET
Wednesday, December 4 • 10:00 AM – 6:00 PM ET
Thursday, December 5 • 10:00 AM – 2:00 PM ET

View lots & auction results online at HA.com/5149 and HA.com/5158

BIDDING METHODS:
HERITAGE Live!® Bidding
Bid live on your computer or mobile, anywhere in the world, during the Auction using our HERITAGE Live!® program at HA.com/Live

Live Floor Bidding
Bid in person during the floor sessions.

Live Telephone Bidding (floor sessions only)
Phone bidding must be arranged on or before Wednesday, December 4, by 12:00 PM CT.
Client Service: 866-835-3243.

Internet Bidding
Internet absentee bidding ends at 10:00 PM CT the evening before each session. HA.com/5149 & HA.com/5158

Fax Bidding
Fax bids must be received on or before Wednesday, December 4, by 12:00 PM CT. Fax: 214-409-1425

Mail Bidding
Mail bids must be received on or before Wednesday, December 4.

Phone: 214.528.3500 • 877-HERITAGE (437-4824)
Fax: 214.409.1425
Direct Client Service Line: 866.835.3243
Email: Bid@HA.com

Fine & Decorative Arts Department Specialists

Steve Ivy
CEO
Co-Chairman of the Board

Jim Halperin
Co-Chairman of the Board

Greg Rohan
President

Paul Minshull
Chief Operating Officer

Todd Imhof
Executive Vice President

Ed Beardsley
Vice President and
Managing Director,
Fine and Decorative Arts

Ed Jaster
Senior Vice President
Heritage Auctions

Brian Roughton
Director, American &
European Art

Aviva Lehmann
Consignment Director,
Fine Arts

Ariana Hartsock
Consignment Director,
Fine Arts

Marianne Berardi, Ph.D.
Senior Expert, Fine Art

3500 Maple Avenue • Dallas, Texas 75219
Phone 214-528-3500 • 877-HERITAGE (437-4824)
HA.com/FineArt

Consignment Directors: Brian Roughton, Aviva Lehmann, Ariana Hartsock
Marianne Berardi, Ph.D.

Cataloged by: Natalie Jones

Table of Contents

Session One	7
The Art of New York	
Session Two	
Property From A Distinguished Dallas Collection	47
American Paintings, Drawings & Sculpture	79
Terms & Conditions	198
How to Ship Your Purchase	201
Index	210
Specialists	212
Auction Calendar	214

It is with great enthusiasm and anticipation that we present our American Art auction in New York. Coinciding with the centennial anniversary of the seminal 1913 Armory show – which introduced New York to Modern Art—what better way to celebrate and give tribute to our great city than with a specialized section devoted to New York.

The Art of New York tells the story of New York City through painting, drawing, watercolor, photography, and memorabilia. With highlights including an iconic Guy Wiggins depiction of Trinity Church, a Berenice Abbott newsstand photograph, and an Annie Leibovitz portrait of Mrs. Brooke Astor in her apartment, *The Art of New York* is wonderfully diverse.

Diversity has always been New York City's strength. Art historian Dr. Ilene Susan Fort once noted that for early 20th century American artists, Modernity meant not a fixed set of forms or systems of theory, but "openness toward subject matter, style, cultural ideas and personal beliefs and attitudes." Dr. Fort's description does certainly apply to not only Modern Art but to our beloved city. Enjoy New York, and enjoy our offerings.

Aviva Lehmann

THE ART OF NEW YORK

SESSION ONE

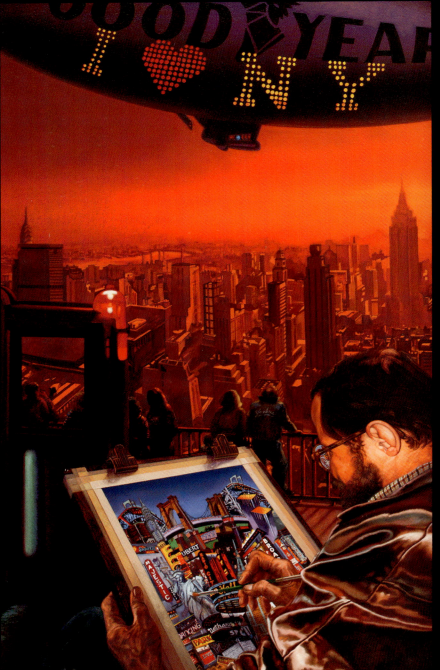

65001

WILLIAM L. HANEY (American, 1939-1992)
A Self-Portrait with Reservations, 1985
Oil on canvas
42 x 26 inches (106.7 x 66.0 cm)
Signed, titled, and dated verso with artist's copyright
Wm. L. Haney / Self-Portrait / with Reservations / 6/85 / ©

PROVENANCE:
Sherry French Gallery, Inc., New York;
Acquired by the present owner from the above, 1986.

EXHIBITED:
Sherry French Gallery, Inc., New York, "William L. Haney: Recent Paintings and Works on Paper," New York, September 3-27, 1986, no. 11.

William L. Haney is renowned for his narrative-realist paintings that focus on depictions of city life, often utilizing an atmospheric, magic-realist light as seen in *A Self-Portrait with Reservations*. In his series of urban narratives, Haney finds a context in which public interest issues intersect with private lives. This edge provides the persistent core of the artist's works, which are often ambitious in size, complexity, and technical achievement.

A Self-Portrait with Reservations is Haney's satirical homage to New York. It is both a good-bye and a love letter to the place he loved, where he felt at home, but could no longer afford. With his usual sense of humor and irony, Haney portrays himself painting a copy of a pop-up postcard commonly purchased by tourists in many of the souvenir shops around New York. The postcard is a pun on Pop Art, as is the blimp in the sky's "pop" symbol. The work captures Haney's mixed emotions about leaving his beloved city through his use of warm, glowing colors, and is one of the most ambitious masterworks from the artist's *oeuvre*.

A Self-Portrait with Reservations was featured in Haney's one-man exhibition at Sherry French Gallery, New York in 1986 and was used as the gallery announcement for the exhibition. Haney's artwork is in the permanent collection of the Metropolitan Museum of Art, New York; The Guggenheim Art Museum, New York; The Butler Art Museum, Youngstown, Ohio, and Greenville Museum of Art, Greenville, South Carolina, among others. At the time of the 1986 exhibition, Haney's artwork was being actively purchased by institutions nationwide. Reviews of Haney's work have appeared in the *New York Times, Art in America,* and *ARTNews*.

Haney's career was cut short when he died at the age of 52 in 1993, at the height of his artistic powers. Shortly thereafter the Mulvane Art Museum in Topeka, Kansas was gifted many paintings by the artist's family to form a core, permanent collection of his artwork. This is a rare opportunity to acquire a *tour-de-force* from Haney's best and most important period.

Estimate: $3,000-$5,000

55002

CARLOS NADAL (Spanish/French, 1917-1998)
Port de New York, circa 1980
Oil on canvas
21-1/4 x 25-3/4 inches (54.0 x 65.4 cm)
Signed lower right: *C. Nadal*
Signed and stamped with artist's atelier stamp verso: *Port de New York / Nadal*

PROPERTY OF A DISTINGUISHED PRIVATE COLLECTOR

PROVENANCE:
Sala Pares, Barcelona, Spain;
Acquired by the present owner from the above.

Estimate: $15,000-$25,000

55003
HUGH FERRISS (American, 1889-1962)
Columbus Circle at Night
Charcoal on paper
14-1/2 x 23 inches (36.8 x 58.4 cm) (sheet)
Signed lower center: *Ferriss*

Estimate: $1,000-$1,500

55004
HUGH FERRISS (American, 1889-1962)
New York at Night
Charcoal on paper
13-1/4 x 22-3/4 inches (33.7 x 57.8 cm) (sheet)
Signed lower left: *Hugh Ferriss*

Estimate: $1,000-$1,500

65005

ROSALYN BODYCOMB (American, b. 1958)
Winter, Brooklyn, 2003
Oil on linen
24-3/4 x 33 inches (62.9 x 83.8 cm)

PROVENANCE:
Mulcahy Modern, Dallas (label verso).

Estimate: $8,000-$12,000

65006
IRVING UNDERHILL (American, 1872-1960)
Grand Central Station at Mid-Day
Vintage gelatin silver print
9-3/4 x 7-3/8 inches (24.8 x 18.7 cm)
Signed in pencil and typewritten inscription *NY 109 - U.S.A. NEW YORK New York / In the Grand Central Station at mid-day.* with artist's stamp and Publisher Photo Service Copyright stamp on verso

Estimate: $1,500-$2,500

65007
GEORGE DANIELL (American, 1911-2002)
Grand Central Station, circa 1938
Gelatin silver, printed 2001
13-1/8 x 7-7/8 inches (33.5 x 20 cm)
Signed in ink; titled, dated, and editioned 9/20 in pencil, with artist's copyright stamp 1997, in association with Sarah Morthland Gallery and Vincent Cianni, N.Y.C. verso

Estimate: $800-$1,200

65008

GEORGE DANIELL (American, 1911-2002)
Subway Near Macy's, 1939
Gelatin silver, printed 1998
13-1/4 x 8-3/4 inches (33.7 x 22.2 cm)
Signed, titled, dated, and editioned 9/20 in ink and artist's copyright stamp 1997, in association with Sarah Morthland Gallery and Vincent Cianni, N.Y.C verso

Estimate: $800-$1,200

5009

ANONYMOUS (20th Century)
Untitled (Broadway), 1952
Gelatin silver
15-1/2 x 19-1/2 inches (39.4 x 49.5 cm)

Estimate: $800-$1,200

65010

LOUIS FAURER (American, 1916-2001)
Times Square, NYC, 1947
Gelatin silver, printed later
12-7/8 x 8-1/2 inches (32.7 x 21.6 cm)
Signed, titled, dated, and editioned *7/18* in pencil on verso

Estimate: $2,000-$3,000

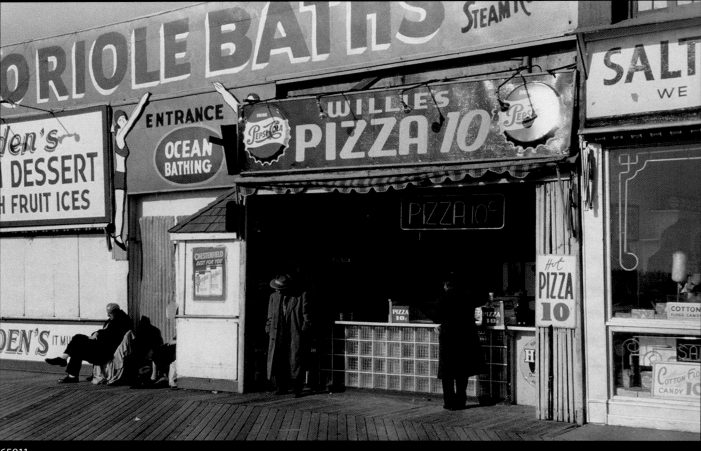

GEORGE DANIELL (American, 1911-2002)
Coney Island, 1950
Gelatin silver, printed 1998
8-3/4 x 13-3/8 inches (22.2 x 34 cm)
Signed in ink; titled, dated, and editioned *9/20* in pencil; and artist's stamp *1997, in association with Sarah Morthland Gallery and Vincent Cianni, N.Y.C.* verso

Estimate: $800-$1,200

65012

CONSUELO KANAGA (American, 1894-1978)
Tug and Barge, East River, circa 1922
Gelatin silver, printed later
2-3/4 x 3-7/8 inches (7.0 x 9.8 cm)
Artist's name and date in unknown hand in pencil on verso

65013
ANONYMOUS (20th Century)
Wall Street, circa 1920
Vintage gelatin silver
8-1/4 x 5 inches (21.0 x 12.7 cm)

Estimate: $800-$1,200

55014
KLAUS SIEBAHN (German, 20th Century)
Park Avenue, New York, 1971
vintage gelatin silver
11 x 15-1/4 inches (27.9 x 38.7 cm)
titled with annotations in pencil and artist's stamps on verso

Estimate: $1,000-$2,000

65015

RUDY BURCKHARDT (American, 1914-1999)
Priscilla Lane, Brooklyn, 1948
Gelatin silver, printed later
6-1/8 x 8 inches (15.5 x 20.3 cm)
Artist's and estate stamps with pencil annotations on verso

Estimate: $2,000-$3,000

55016

BERENICE ABBOTT (American, 1898-1991)
Newsstand, East 32nd Street & Third Avenue, Manhattan, November 19, 1935, 1935
Early gelatin silver
7-1/2 x 9-1/2 inches (19.1 x 24.1 cm)
Artist's stamp *photograph / berenice abbott / 55 w. 53rd st. / new york city* on the verso

Estimate: $3,000-$5,000

65017

AMERICAN SCHOOL (20th Century)
New York Yacht Club Resolution, 1930
Pen and ink on paper
15 x 11 inches (38.1 x 27.9 cm) (sight)

PROPERTY FORMERLY FROM THE BROOKE ASTOR COLLECTION

Estimate: $300-$500

65018

ANONYMOUS (20th Century)
Astor Family Memorabilia: Four Photographs, Four Letters and Two Prints
Mixed media
12 x 13-1/2 inches (30.5 x 34.3 cm) (largest)

This group of ten items comprises (1) a photograph the Susan B. Wagner wing of Gracie Mansion built by Mott B. Schmidt (also the architect for the townhouse at 124 East 80th Street for Vincent Astor) inscribed to Brooke Astor from Mayor John Lindsay; (2) a photograph of Cardinal Cooke presenting an award to Brooke Astor, inscribed by the Cardinal to Brooke, together with another inscribed photograph of Cardinal Cooke; (3) a photograph of Victor Astor greeting clergy at the Astor Children's Home in Rhinebeck, New York; (4) a photograph of Nancy Reagan and C. Douglas Dillon, former Ambassador to France under Eisenhower and Secretary of the Treasury under President John F. Kennedy greeting Brooke Astor, inscribed by Nancy Reagan; (5) a letter and an invitation to Ed Koch's Gala 56th Birthday Celebration, signed and inscribed by Ed Koch; and (6) three signed political letters to Brook Astor from Nelson Rockefeller, Jacob Javits and Mayor Ed Koch.

PROPERTY FORMERLY FROM THE BROOKE ASTOR COLLECTION

Estimate: $200-$300

65019

**ANNIE LEIBOVITZ
(American, b. 1949)**
Brooke Astor, New York, 1997
Chromogenic print
12-1/4 x 16-3/4 inches
(31.1 x 42.5 cm)
Signed, dated, and inscribed in ink in bottom margin: *for Brooke / New York 1997 / Ann Leibovitz*

PROPERTY FORMERLY FROM THE BROOKE ASTOR COLLECTION

Estimate: $1,000-$1,500

65020

CECIL BEATON (British, 1904-1980)
Brooke Astor, 1956
Vintage gelatin silver
9-3/8 x 7-1/2 inches (23.8 x 19.1 cm) (sheet)
Signed in red conte crayon on the mount recto

PROPERTY FORMERLY FROM THE BROOKE ASTOR COLLECTION

Estimate: $400-$600

GUY CARLETON WIGGINS (American, 1883-1962)
Wall Street Storm (Old Trinity, New York), 1956
Oil on canvas
30 x 25 inches (76.2 x 63.5 cm)
Signed lower right: *Guy Wiggins N.A.*
Signed, dated, and inscribed verso: *Wall St. Storm / Feb 1st 1956 / Guy Wiggins N.A.*

NOTE:
This lot is accompanied by a photocopy of the original bill of sale from W.R. Fine Galleries, Dallas.

While in Paris during the summer of 1889, the American Impressionist Childe Hassam likely would have seen Claude Monet's *Rue Montorgueil* depicting the celebration of June 30, 1878, a festival day on which French flags hung from buildings at the Galerie Georges Petit. Hassam's general familiarity with Monet and the other Impressionists prompted him to emulate Monet's *Rue Montorgueil* in his own flag painting from 1889, *Rue Daunou*.

Rue Daunou was not well received in the United States, and Hassam did not return to the flag theme until 1916. His first flag work from 1916, *Just Off the Avenue, Fifty-Third Street* (fig. 1) is an ordinary street scene on a sunny day, resembling his depictions of country life that he painted for most of his career.

Another noted American Impressionist, Guy C. Wiggins, began his career as a landscape painter. He traveled abroad many times, especially in France, and was influenced by the Impressionists. While in Europe, he painted beautiful Impressionist paintings of snowcapped mountains and villages. Like Hassam, he would return to the United States and work in Old Lyme, Connecticut, Cos-Cob, Connecticut, and New York City. They both shared a love for the city. Wiggins painted his first New York City scene in 1912 (fig. 2) from a friend's office on the 26th floor of a skyscraper overlooking three bridges across the East River (Metropolitan Museum collection).

Wiggins was elected an Associate Member of the National Academy of Design in 1916 and an Academician in 1919, among numerous other awards. His works are represented in the United States' most prestigious museum collections.

Estimate: $120,000-$150,000

(fig. 1) ***Just Off the Ave, Fifty-Third Street, 1916***,
Childe Hassam (1859-1935)

(fig. 2) ***Metropolitan Tower, 1912***
By Guy C. Wiggins

65022

AMERICAN SCHOOL (20th Century)
Parade on York Avenue, May 25, 1918
Oil on canvas
16 x 11-1/2 inches (40.6 x 29.2 cm)
Signed indistinctly and dated lower left: *F. F...ct / 25/5 1918*
Inscribed by the artist (verso) in Czech, which in translation reads: *Parade of Czecho-Slovaks in New-York on May 25, 1918 to welcome Professor T[omas]. G[arrigue]. Masaryk (33 up from Ave. A.)*

The present work depicts a parade on York Avenue near the Bohemian National Hall in May of 1918 to welcome Professor Tomas Garrigue Masaryk, the future first President of the independent republic of Czechoslovakia, which was formed in November of the same year. The red and white flags flying alongside the American flag are the original flag for the Czechoslovakian region, which was used until 1920 when the flag was redesigned. Early in 1918 Masaryk had traveled to the United States to convince President Woodrow Wilson to support the cause of Czechoslovak independence from the Austro-Hungarian empire. Prior to this parade in New York on May 25th, Masaryk was in Chicago, which boasted the largest Czech immigrant population in the United States, and where an enormous parade also welcomed him on May 5th. In the present work, the Bohemian National Hall, the major Czech social club in New York, is the building on the right side of the street with the blond stone facade and pronounced cornice.

Estimate: $1,500-$2,500

65023

TORE ASPLUND (American, 1903-1978)
New York Street Scene
Oil on artists' board
18 x 14 inches (45.7 x 35.6 cm)
Signed lower left: *Tore Asplund NA*

Estimate: $500-$700

65024

LAURENCE A. CAMPBELL (American, b. 1939)
January Snow Storm
Oil on canvas
40 x 30 inches (101.6 x 76.2 cm)
Signed lower left: *Laurence A Campbell*
Signed and inscribed verso: *(January Snow Storm) Chestnut St. Phila. Laurence A Campbell 163287*

65025
PAUL CORNOYER (American, 1864-1923)
Early Evening, Empire Park, New York, circa 1910
Oil on canvas
18 x 24 inches (45.7 x 61.0 cm)
Signed lower left: *Paul Cornoyer*

PROPERTY OF A DISTINGUISHED PRIVATE COLLECTOR

PROVENANCE:
Private collection, New York;
Private collection, Ho-Ho-Kus, New Jersey;
Owen Gallery, New York;
Private collection, acquired from the above, 2003;
Hawthorne Fine Art, New York;
Acquired by the present owner from the above, 2009.

Paul Cornoyer is best known for his elegant and atmospheric paintings of turn-of-the-century New York. Born in Saint Louis, Cornoyer began his artistic education at the Saint Louis School of Art, painting in the Barbizon style then in vogue. By 1889 he had saved enough money to study in Paris, where he attended the Académie Julian under Jules-Joseph Lefebvre, Louis Blanc, and Benjamin Constant. Like many students of Constant and Lefebvre, Cornoyer adopted elements of a Tonalist style, but the Impressionists, and later the Ash Can School, also influenced him, especially in his preference for urban scenes. He returned to Saint Louis in 1894 but moved to New York in 1898 at the encouragement of William Merritt Chase. There, Cornoyer associated with the leading artists of the day, including Thomas Wilmer Dewing, John Henry Twachtman, Julian Alden Weir, and Childe Hassam, and made his reputation as a painter of the city's fashionable districts.

Cornoyer often painted views of places that were just a short walk from his studio on West 57th Street, like the Plaza Hotel and Columbus Circle. It was probably on one of these walks that Cornoyer set up his easel at the corner of West 65th Street and Broadway to paint *Early Evening, Empire Park, New York*. Looking southwest past the small triangular park formed by the intersection of Broadway, Columbus Avenue, and West 63rd Street, Cornoyer depicts the old Hotel Empire at 63rd and Broadway on the left, the Ninth Avenue elevated railroad that ran down Columbus on the right, and the Church of Saint Paul the Apostle at 60th and Columbus in the distance. The church and the park (now known as Dante Park) are the only elements of the picture that remain today; the Hotel Empire was rebuilt in 1922, the "El" was dismantled in 1940, and Lincoln Center was built from 1962 to 1968 where the buildings on the right stood.

Early Evening, Empire Park, New York shows the clear stylistic influence of the Ash Can School, although Cornoyer retains an emphasis on the atmosphere of the scene rather than on its subject matter. The trees and architectural forms silhouetted against the fading daylight are an enduring Tonalist element in Cornoyer's style, and this effect, along with the expressive brushwork in the sky, gives the painting much of its power. But true to his urban subject, Cornoyer depicts the band of electric lights at street level, and he includes four figures crossing Broadway, perhaps on their way home from the 66th Street "El" stop. One of Cornoyer's most artistic works, *Early Evening, Empire Park, New York* surpasses his typical New York scenes in its successful synthesis of styles and its strong mood.

Estimate: $50,000-$70,000

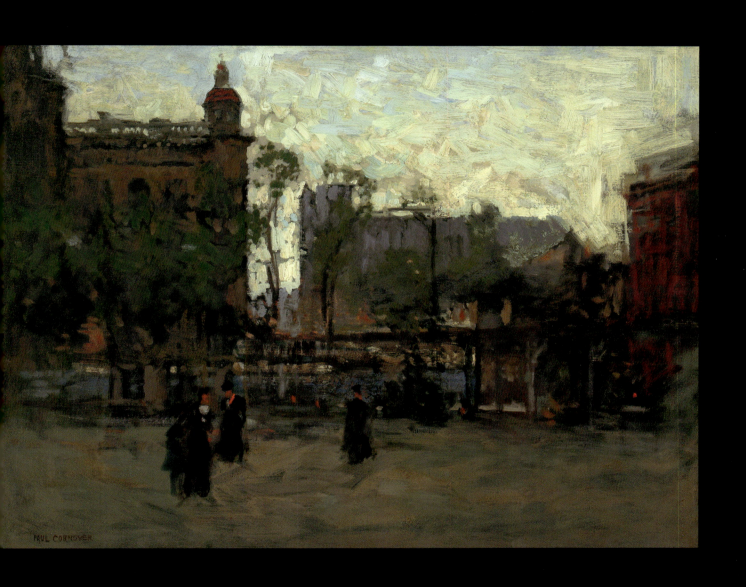

65026

GUY CARLETON WIGGINS (American, 1883-1962)
The Library, 5th Avenue, circa 1940
Oil on canvas
20-1/4 x 24-1/4 inches (51.4 x 61.6 cm)
Signed lower left: *Guy Wiggins*
Titled and signed verso: *The Library / 5th Avenue / Guy Wiggins N.A.*

PROVENANCE:
Private collection, Dallas.

We wish to thank Mr. Guy A. Wiggins for his gracious assistance in cataloguing this painting. In his letter of authenticity, which accompanies this lot, Mr. Wiggins writes, "I believe it was painted between 1936 when [my father] became a National Academician and 1952 when double-deckers of the type shown here were withdrawn from service."

Estimate: $30,000-$50,000

65027
GUY CARLETON WIGGINS (American, 1883-1962)
Just Off 5th Avenue at 53rd Street (à la Childe Hassam), 1939
Oil on canvas
28 x 23-1/2 inches
(71.1 x 59.7 cm)
Signed lower right: *Guy Wiggins*
Signed, dated, and inscribed verso: *Guy Wiggins 1939 / N.J. / "a la Ch. Hassam"*

PROVENANCE:
Kenny Lux Gallery, New York;
Christie's, New York, *Important American Paintings, Drawings & Sculpture*, December 5, 1986, lot 199;
Christie's, New York, *Important American Paintings, Drawings & Sculpture*, May 18, 2004, lot 104;
Roughton Galleries, Dallas, 2004;
Private collection, Houston.

In *Just Off 5th Avenue at 53rd Street (À la Childe Hassam)* Guy C. Wiggins depicts an oblique view from the southeast corner of 53rd Street and Sixth Avenue, looking toward Fifth Avenue. St. Thomas Episcopal Church's looming gray tower is contrasted against a bright blue sky and pastel yellow-and-green foliage on a crisp spring day. Painted in 1939, the painting commemorates the opening of New York's Museum of Modern Art in May of that year.

Just Off 5th Avenue at 53rd Street (À La Childe Hassam) is also Guy Wiggins' tribute to America's foremost flag painter, Childe Hassam (1859-1935), who had visited this same corner on May 13, 1916. Before the United States entered World War I, New York City periodically decorated with flags to mark special occasions. Hassam stated that it was the celebration of Preparedness Day on May 13, 1916, that inspired his first flag painting, *Just Off the Avenue, Fifty-Third Street, May 1916*.

Estimate: $80,000-$120,000

65028

GUY CARLETON WIGGINS (American, 1883-1962)
Financial Center
Oil on canvas
24-1/4 x 20-1/4 inches (61.6 x 51.4 cm)
Signed lower left: *Guy Wiggins NA*
Signed and titled verso: *Financial Center / Guy Wiggins*

Estimate: $30,000-$40,000

65029
GEORGE COPELAND AULT (American, 1891-1948)
42nd Street from Bryant Park, 1920
pencil on paper
8-1/8 x 5-7/8 inches (20.7 x 15.0 cm)
signed and dated lower left: *G.C.A '20*

PROVENANCE:
Mrs. George Ault;
James Graham & Sons, New York;
Vanderwoude Tannanbaum Gallery, New York;
Grand Central Art Galleries, New York;
Private collection, New York.

EXHIBITED:
New York, Whitney Museum of American Art, "George Ault Nocturnes," December 6, 1973-January 6, 1974;
New York, Grand Central Art Galleries, New York, "Empire City in an Age of Urbanism 1875-1945," December 14, 1988-January 26, 1989.

Estimate: $5,000-$7,000

65030
JOSEPH PENNELL
(American, 1857-1926)
New York Harbor
watercolor on paper
10-1/4 x 11-1/2 inches
(26.0 x 29.2 cm)
signed lower left: *Pennell*

PROVENANCE:
Private collection, New York.

Estimate: $4,000-$6,000

65031

EZRA WINTER (American, 1886-1949)
The Pulitzer Fountain, Grand Army Plaza, Manhattan, 1919
Watercolor on paper
20 x 29 inches (50.8 x 73.7 cm) (sheet)
Signed and dated lower right: *Ezra Winter 1919*

A native of Manistee, Michigan, Ezra Winter studied at the Chicago College of Fine Arts in 1908 and 1909 before winning the American Academy in Rome scholarship in 1911. While in Europe, Winter broadened his scope by observing and exploring a combination of technical practices, concentrating on the disciplines and techniques of mural painting.

Having traveled extensively, Winter made a decision to return to the United States. He set up a studio in New York City where he produced renderings of his surroundings, of which the present work is a stellar example.

Winter was extremely successful in his lifetime. He was unanimously elected to full membership of the American National Academy in 1924 and he was an active member of the National Society of Mural Painters. Winter's works were commissioned and displayed in some of the most prominent institutions throughout New York including The Cunard Building, Rockefeller Center, the New York Cotton Exchange and Radio City Music Hall.

Estimate: $5,000-$7,000

55032

YVONNE TWINING (American, 1907-2004)
Waterfront, 1939
Oil on canvas
22 x 28 inches (55.9 x 71.1 cm)
Signed and dated lower left: *Yvonne Twining '39*
Inscribed verso: *W.P.A 1939 / Medium: Oil on canvas / Size: 22 x 28" / Title: "Waterfront" / Finished: August 30, 1939 / Artist: Yvonne Twining*

Estimate: $2,000-$3,000

55033
GUY CARLETON WIGGINS (American, 1883-1962)
The French Warship "Richelieu" in the East River, 1943
Oil on canvas board
8-1/4 x 10 inches (21.0 x 25.4 cm)
Signed lower left: *Guy Wiggins N.A.*; dated lower right: *1943*
Inscribed verso: *The French Warship "Richelieu" in the East River / To my son, Carleton. / Apr. 1943. / Guy Wiggins. NA.*

PROVENANCE:
The artist;
Carleton Wiggins, the artist's son, gift from above, 1943;
Mr. Katler, 2002;
Private collection, Gulfport, Mississippi.

This lot is accompanied by a copy of a 2002 letter from the artist's granddaughter, Susan Sokol, stating that "this painting was given to my father Carleton Wiggins from my grandfather Guy Wiggins."

Estimate: $10,000-$12,000

65034

SAMUEL ROTHBORT (Russian/American, 1882-1971)
Lower East Side (View of Tompkins Square Park), 1947
Oil on canvas
30 x 36 inches (76.2 x 91.4 cm)
Signed lower right: S Rothbort

PROVENANCE:
Shannon's Fine Art Auctioneers, Milford, Connecticut, October 25, 2001, lot 136;
Private collector, New York, acquired from the above.

65035

**SAMUEL ROTHBORT
(Russian/American, 1882-1971)**
Alphabet City, New York
Oil on canvas
24 x 36 inches (61.0 x 91.4 cm)
Signed lower center: *S. Rothbort*

Estimate: $4,000-$6,000

65036

SAMUEL ROTHBORT (Russian/American, 1882-1971)
Christmas Cactus, circa 1940s
oil on canvas
30 x 36 inches (76.2 x 91.4 cm)
Signed lower right: *S. Rothbort*

PROVENANCE:
Private collector, New York.

The present work depicts a view of Brooklyn from the artist's studio.

Estimate: $2,500-$3,500

65037
ROBERT HENRI (American, 1865-1929)
Isadora Duncan and *At the Opera (two works)*, 1904
Conte crayon on paper; charcoal on paper
18 x 12 inches (45.7 x 30.5 cm) (sight of larger)
Each bears estate stamp 'RH'; the second dated lower left: *1904*

PROPERTY OF A DISTINGUISHED PRIVATE COLLECTOR

PROVENANCE:
Hirschl & Adler Galleries, New York;
Donald Brenwasser, acquired from the above, *circa* 1964;
Estate of the above;
Sotheby's, New York, September 24, 2008, lot 10;
Acquired by the present owner from the above.

Estimate: $4,000-$6,000

65038
NELL BRINKLEY (American, 1886-1944)
The New Year, 1914-15
Pen and ink on paper
19-1/2 x 13-1/4 inches (49.5 x 33.7 cm) (sight)
Signed lower center: *Nell Brinkley*

Estimate: $1,200-$1,800

65040

GEORGE SCHWACHA (American, 1908-1986)
New York City Scene
Oil on artists' board
19-1/2 x 20 inches (49.5 x 50.8 cm)
Signed lower left: *Geo Schwacha*

Estimate: $800-$1,200

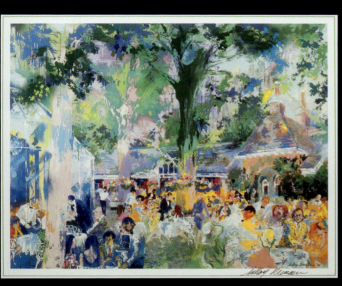

65039

LEROY NEIMAN (American, b. 1926)
Tavern on the Green, 1991
Color lithograph
14-5/8 x 18-1/4 inches (37.1 x 46.4 cm) (image)
Signed in pen: *Leroy Neiman*
Signed and dated in plate lower right: *Leroy Neiman '91*

Estimate: $500-$700

65041

GEORGE SCHWACHA (American, 1908-1986)
Vegetable Stand, New York
Watercolor and ink on paper
18 x 22 inches (45.7 x 55.9 cm) (sight)
Signed lower left: *Geo Schwacha*

Estimate: $500-$700

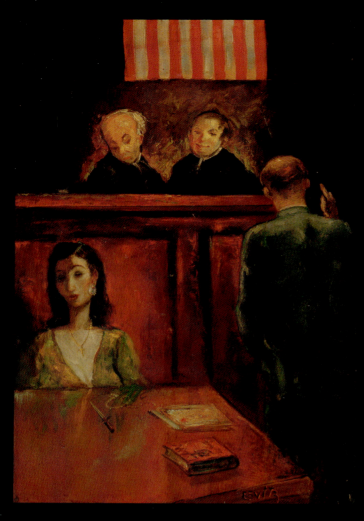

65042

JACK LEVITZ (American, 20th Century)
Trial Scene, Attorney and Dark Haired Woman with Necklace and Dagger Before Judges
Oil on board
20 x 14 inches (50.8 x 35.6 cm)
Signed lower right: *Levitz*

PROPERTY FORMERLY FROM THE ESTATE OF JACK LEVITZ

Estimate: $1,500-$2,000

65043

JACK LEVITZ (American, 20th Century)
Dancer in Gold Costume Before Three Judges
Oil on canvasboard
16 x 12 inches (40.6 x 30.5 cm)
Signed lower right: *Levitz*

PROPERTY FORMERLY FROM THE ESTATE OF JACK LEVITZ

Estimate: $1,500-$2,000

65044

JACK LEVITZ
(American, 20th Century)
Trial Scene, Performers and Attorney Before Three Judges
Oil on canvas
24 x 30 inches (61.0 x 76.2 cm)
Signed lower left: *Levitz*

PROPERTY FORMERLY FROM THE ESTATE OF JACK LEVITZ

Estimate: $1,500-$2,000

65045

JACK LEVITZ
(American, 20th Century)
Circus Performers on Trial Before Three Judges
Oil on canvas
32 x 36 inches (81.3 x 91.4 cm)
Signed lower right: *Levitz*

PROPERTY FORMERLY FROM THE ESTATE OF JACK LEVITZ

Estimate: $1,500-$2,000

64001

JOHN JAMES AUDUBON (American, 1785-1851)
Florida Cormorant or Double-crested Cormorant (Phalacrocorax auritus), 1835
Plate CCLII from *The Birds of America*
Hand-colored engraving with aquatint and etching on J. Whatman Turkey Mill dated 1835
Plate: 19-3/4 x 26-1/4 inches (50.2 x 66.7 cm)
Sheet: 25-7/8 x 38-3/8 inches (65.7 x 97.5 cm)
Engraved, printed, and colored by R. Havell, London

Estimate: $3,000-$5,000

65044

**JACK LEVITZ
(American, 20th Century)**
Trial Scene, Performers and Attorney Before Three Judges
Oil on canvas
24 x 30 inches (61.0 x 76.2 cm)
Signed lower left: *Levitz*

PROPERTY FORMERLY FROM THE ESTATE OF JACK LEVITZ

Estimate: $1,500-$2,000

65045

**JACK LEVITZ
(American, 20th Century)**
Circus Performers on Trial Before Three Judges
Oil on canvas
32 x 36 inches (81.3 x 91.4 cm)
Signed lower right: *Levitz*

PROPERTY FORMERLY FROM THE ESTATE OF JACK LEVITZ

Estimate: $1,500-$2,000

65046

JACK LEVITZ
(American, 20th Century)
Burlesque Stage Show
Oil on canvas
23 x 28 inches (58.4 x 71.1 cm)
Signed lower right: *Levitz*

PROPERTY FORMERLY FROM THE ESTATE OF JACK LEVITZ

Estimate: $1,500-$2,000

65047

JACK LEVITZ (American, 20th Century)
Burlesque Performer
Oil on canvas
36 x 26 inches (91.4 x 66.0 cm)
Signed upper right: *Levitz*

PROPERTY FORMERLY FROM THE ESTATE OF JACK LEVITZ

Estimate: $1,500-$2,000

End of Session One

BIRDS OF AMERICA;

from

ORIGINAL DRAWINGS

by

JOHN JAMES AUDUBON,

*Fellow of the Royal Societies of London & Edinburgh and of the
Linnean & Zoological Societies of London
Member of the Natural History Society of Paris, of the Lyceum of New York,
&c. &c. &c.*

London.

Published by the Author.

1827—30.

Heritage Auctions is pleased to offer forty-three magnificent hand-colored engravings from John James Audubon's ornithological magnum opus, The Birds of America; from Original Drawings. *Published between 1827-38 in an edition of around 200,* The Birds of America *represents the culmination of Audubon's life work as a naturalist-artist, depicting in 435 plates every bird species from North America. In order to feature the birds as life-size, Audubon insisted that the engravings be printed on "double-elephant" broadsheets measuring 39 ½ x 26 ½", about twice the size of the drawing paper on which he made the original watercolor studies. Assembled by a single owner from Dallas, the present forty-three examples exhibit strong impressions with crisp plate-marks; they also capture a sampling of the hundreds of species from the folio, notably seabirds (for instance, cormorants, razor bills, sandpipers, and terns) and songbirds (including finches, larks, sparrows, and warblers).*

Audubon's path to becoming the world's greatest bird painter was circuitous, if not serendipitous. Born in 1785 in Les Cayes, Santo Domingo, the illegitimate son of a French sea captain and his Creole mistress, Jean-Jacques Fougère Audubon grew up in Nantes, France. It was here that he developed his passion for birds, collecting countryside specimens that he would stuff, display, and illustrate. To prevent his son's conscription in the Napoleonic Wars, Jean Audubon sent him in 1803 to a farm he had recently purchased outside of Philadelphia, where young Audubon (having anglicized his name to John James) preferred collecting birds to running the family's mining business. Five years later, Audubon and his Pennsylvania bride, Lucy Bakewell, settled in Kentucky, and he cobbled together jobs as a merchant, miller, and portrait painter. All the while, he feverishly studied and rendered birds, creating a system of suspending specimens from wires as a means of simulating lifelike poses. His discovery of new bird species on trips during the early 1820s through Mississippi, Louisiana, Alabama, and Florida convinced him to compile an illustrated book of native birds, despite his flimsy fortune and Lucy's hardship as the family breadwinner.

Unable to find a publisher in Philadelphia for his proposed book of bird drawings, Audubon traveled to England and Scotland in 1826 in search of support. Abroad, he met luminaries in the scientific community, including the botanist William Roscoe, who helped him exhibit his drawings in Manchester; the ornithologist William Swainson; the naturalist William MacGillivray, who later edited the text for The Birds of America; *and William Home Lizars, an engraver in Edinburgh who, impressed by Audubon's work, agreed to print the massive folio. However, when Lizars was able only to complete the first ten plates, Audubon approached the established London engraver Robert Havell, who together with his son Robert, Jr., took up the project. Ultimately,* The Birds of America *was issued serially in five-plate sets, for a total of 435 plates, over the course of a decade.*

Even today, scholars and collectors worldwide consider The Birds of America *a masterwork, if not the masterwork, of ornithological study. Approximately 200 copies were published during the 1830s, and around 119 of these remain in complete form today. Of these, most reside in museums, universities, and libraries, with only a handful in private collections. Both complete and partial copies have been sold at auction since 1973, but only rarely. These present impressions are exceptional examples that are fresh to the market.*

64001

JOHN JAMES AUDUBON (American, 1785-1851)
Florida Cormorant or Double-crested Cormorant (Phalacrocorax auritus), 1835
Plate CCLII from *The Birds of America*
Hand-colored engraving with aquatint and etching on J. Whatman Turkey Mill dated 1835
Plate: 19-3/4 x 26-1/4 inches (50.2 x 66.7 cm)
Sheet: 25-7/8 x 38-3/8 inches (65.7 x 97.5 cm)
Engraved, printed, and colored by R. Havell, London

Estimate: $3,000-$5,000

64002

JOHN JAMES AUDUBON (American, 1785-1851)
Great Esquimaux Curlew or Whimbrel (Numenius phaeopus), 1835
Plate CCXXXVII from *The Birds of America*
Hand-colored engraving with aquatint and etching on J. Whatman Turkey Mill dated 1834
Plate: 20-5/8 x 25-5/8 inches (52.4 x 65.1 cm)
Sheet: 25-7/8 x 38-1/2 inches (65.7 x 97.8 cm)
Engraved, printed, and colored by R. Havell, London

Estimate: $5,000-$7,000

64003

JOHN JAMES AUDUBON (American, 1785-1851)
Common Cormorant or Great Cormorant (Phalacrocorax carbo), 1835
Plate CCLXVI from *The Birds of America*
Hand-colored engraving with aquatint and etching on J. Whatman dated 1835
Plate: 25-1/2 x 38 inches (64.8 x 96.5 cm)
Sheet: 25-7/8 x 38-5/8 inches (65.7 x 98.1 cm)
Engraved, printed, and colored by R. Havell, London

Estimate: $3,000-$5,000

64004

JOHN JAMES AUDUBON (American, 1785-1851)
Double-crested Cormorant (Phalacrocorax auritus), 1835
Plate CCLVII from *The Birds of America*
Hand-colored engraving with aquatint and etching on J. Whatman dated 1834
Plate: 30-1/8 x 21-3/8 inches (76.5 x 54.3 cm)
Sheet: 38-1/2 x 25-7/8 inches (97.8 x 65.7 cm)
Engraved, printed, and colored by R. Havell, London

Estimate: $2,000-$3,000

64005

JOHN JAMES AUDUBON (American, 1785-1851)
Bachmans Finch or Bachman's Sparrow (Aimophila aestivalis), 1833
Plate CLXV from *The Birds of America*
Hand-colored engraving with aquatint and etching on J. Whatman dated 1833
Plate: 19-1/4 x 12-1/8 inches (48.9 x 30.8 cm)
Sheet: 38-3/8 x 25-3/4 inches (97.5 x 65.4 cm)
Engraved, printed, and colored by R. Havell, London

Estimate: $1,500-$2,500

64006

JOHN JAMES AUDUBON (American, 1785-1851)
Rice Bird or Bobolink (Dolichonyx oryzivorus)
Plate LIV from *The Birds of America*
Hand-colored engraving with aquatint and etching on J. Whatman dated 1832
Plate: 19-3/8 x 12-1/8 inches (49.2 x 30.8 cm)
Sheet: 37-7/8 x 25-5/8 inches (96.2 x 65.1 cm)
Engraved, printed, and colored by R. Havell, London

Estimate: $1,500-$2,500

64007

JOHN JAMES AUDUBON (American, 1785-1851)
Black & Yellow Warbler or Magnolia Warbler (Dendroica magnolia)
Plate L from *The Birds of America*
Hand-colored engraving with aquatint and etching on J. Whatman dated 1832
Plate: 19-1/4 x 12-1/8 inches (48.9 x 30.8 cm)
Sheet: 37-7/8 x 25-1/2 inches (96.2 x 64.8 cm)
Engraved, printed, and colored by R. Havell, London

Estimate: $1,000-$1,500

64008

JOHN JAMES AUDUBON (American, 1785-1851)
Traill's Fly-catcher or Willow Flycatcher (Empidonax traillii)
Plate XLV from The Birds of America
Hand-colored engraving with aquatint and etching on J. Whatman dated 1832
Plate: 19-3/8 x 12-1/8 inches (49.2 x 30.8 cm)
Sheet: 37-7/8 x 29-5/8 inches (96.2 x 75.2 cm)
Engraved, printed, and colored by R. Havell, London

Estimate: $1,200-$1,500

64009

JOHN JAMES AUDUBON (American, 1785-1851)
Snow Bird or Dark-eyed Junco (Fringilla hyemalis)
Plate XIII from *The Birds of America*
Hand-colored engraving with aquatint and etching on J. Whatman dated 1832
Plate: 19-1/2 x 12-1/4 inches (49.5 x 31.1 cm)
Sheet: 38-1/8 x 25-5/8 inches (96.8 x 65.1 cm)
Engraved, printed, and colored by R. Havell, London

Estimate: $1,000-$2,000

64010

JOHN JAMES AUDUBON (American, 1785-1851)
Pine Finch or Pine Siskin (Carduelis pinus), 1833
Plate CLXXX from *The Birds of America*
Hand-colored engraving with aquatint and etching on J. Whatman dated 1833
Plate: 19-3/8 x 12-1/4 inches (49.2 x 31.1 cm)
Sheet: 38-1/8 x 25-3/4 inches (96.8 x 65.4 cm)
Engraved, printed, and colored by R. Havell, London

Estimate: $800-$1,200

64011

JOHN JAMES AUDUBON (American, 1785-1851)
Sharp-tailed Finch or Saltmarsh Sharp-tailed Sparrow (Ammodramus caudacutus), 1832
Plate CXLIX from *The Birds of America*
Hand-colored engraving with aquatint and etching on J. Whatman dated 1832
Plate: 19-1/8 x 12 inches (48.6 x 30.5 cm)
Sheet: 37-7/8 x 25-3/4 inches (96.2 x 65.4 cm)
Engraved, printed, and colored by R. Havell, London

Estimate: $1,500-$2,500

64012

JOHN JAMES AUDUBON (American, 1785-1851)
White Bellied Swallow or Marsh Wren (Cistothorus palustris)
Plate XCVIII from *The Birds of America*
Hand-colored engraving with aquatint and etching on J. Whatman dated 1832
Plate: 19-1/4 x 12-1/8 inches (48.9 x 30.8 cm)
Sheet: 37-3/4 x 25-3/8 inches (95.9 x 64.5 cm)
Engraved, printed, and colored by R. Havell, London

Estimate: $800-$1,200

64013

JOHN JAMES AUDUBON (American, 1785-1851)
Sooty Tern (Sterna fuscata), 1834
Plate CCXXXV from *The Birds of America*
Hand-colored engraving with aquatint and etching on J. Whatman Turkey Mill dated 1834
Plate: 12-1/4 x 19-3/8 inches (31.1 x 49.2 cm)
Sheet: 25-7/8 x 38-3/8 inches (65.7 x 97.5 cm)
Engraved, printed, and colored by R. Havell, London

Estimate: $800-$1,200

64014

JOHN JAMES AUDUBON (American, 1785-1851)
American Swift or Chimney Swift (Chaetura pelagica), 1833
Plate CLVIII from *The Birds of America*
Hand-colored engraving with aquatint and etching on J. Whatman Turkey Mill dated 1832
Plate: 19-1/2 x 12-1/4 inches (49.5 x 31.1 cm)
Sheet: 38-3/8 x 25-5/8 inches (97.5 x 65.1 cm)
Engraved, printed, and colored by R. Havell, London

Estimate: $3,000-$5,000

64015

JOHN JAMES AUDUBON (American, 1785-1851)
Blue Yellow-back Warbler or Northern Parula (Parula americana)
Plate XV from *The Birds of America*
Hand-colored engraving with aquatint and etching on J. Whatman dated 1832
Plate: 19-1/4 x 12 inches (48.9 x 30.5 cm)
Sheet: 37-7/8 x 25-3/8 inches (96.2 x 64.5 cm)
Engraved, printed, and colored by R. Havell, London

Estimate: $1,500-$2,500

64016

JOHN JAMES AUDUBON (American, 1785-1851)
Prarie Warbler (Dendrioca discolor)
Plate XIV from *The Birds of America*
Hand-colored engraving with aquatint and etching on J. Whatman dated 1832
Plate: 19-1/4 x 12 inches (48.9 x 30.5 cm)
Sheet: 37-3/4 x 25-1/2 inches (95.9 x 64.8 cm)
Engraved, printed, and colored by R. Havell, London

Estimate: $800-$1,200

64017
JOHN JAMES AUDUBON (American, 1785-1851)
Bewick's Long Tailed Wren or Bewick's Wren (Thryomanes bewickii)
Plate XVIII from *The Birds of America*
Hand-colored engraving with aquatint and etching on J. Whatman dated 1831
Plate: 19-3/4 x 12-1/4 inches (50.2 x 31.1 cm)
Sheet: 38-1/8 x 25-3/4 inches (96.8 x 65.4 cm)
Engraved, printed, and colored by R. Havell, London

Estimate: $800-$1,200

64018
JOHN JAMES AUDUBON (American, 1785-1851)
Hermit Thrush (Catharus guttatus)
Plate LVIII from *The Birds of America*
Hand-colored engraving with aquatint and etching on J. Whatman dated 1832
Plate: 19-1/2 x 12 inches (49.5 x 30.5 cm)
Sheet: 38-1/4 x 25-5/8 inches (97.2 x 65.1 cm)
Engraved, printed, and colored by R. Havell, London

Estimate: $1,000-$1,500

64019

JOHN JAMES AUDUBON (American, 1785-1851)
Golden-crested-Wren or Golden-crowned Kinglet (Regulus satrapa)
Plate CLXXXIII from *The Birds of America*
Hand-colored engraving with aquatint and etching on J. Whatman dated 1833
Plate: 19-1/4 x 12 inches (48.9 x 30.5 cm)
Sheet: 38-3/8 x 25-3/4 inches (97.5 x 65.4 cm)
Engraved, printed, and colored by R. Havell, London

Estimate: $800-$1,200

64020

JOHN JAMES AUDUBON (American, 1785-1851)
Indigo-bird or Indigo Bunting (Passerina cyanea)
Plate LXXIV from *The Birds of America*
Hand-colored engraving with aquatint and etching on J. Whatman dated 1832
Plate: 19-3/8 x 12-1/8 inches (49.2 x 30.8 cm)
Sheet: 37-7/8 x 25-1/2 inches (96.2 x 64.8 cm)
Engraved, printed, and colored by R. Havell, London

Estimate: $1,000-$1,500

64021

JOHN JAMES AUDUBON (American, 1785-1851)
Pewit Flycatcher or Eastern Phoebe (Sayornis phoebe)
Plate CXX from *The Birds of America*
Hand-colored engraving with aquatint and etching on J. Whatman dated 1834
Plate: 19-1/2 x 12-1/4 inches (49.5 x 31.1 cm)
Sheet: 38-1/8 x 25-7/8 inches (96.8 x 65.7 cm)
Engraved, printed, and colored by R. Havell, London

Estimate: $800-$1,200

64022

JOHN JAMES AUDUBON (American, 1785-1851)
Chipping Sparrow (Spizella passerina)
Plate CIV from *The Birds of America*
Hand-colored engraving with aquatint and etching on J. Whatman dated 1830
Plate: 19-1/2 x 12-1/8 inches (49.5 x 30.8 cm)
Sheet: 38-5/8 x 26 inches (98.1 x 66.0 cm)
Engraved, printed, and colored by R. Havell Jr., London

Estimate: $600-$800

64023

JOHN JAMES AUDUBON (American, 1785-1851)
Hemlock Warbler or Blackburnian Warbler, 1832
Plate CXXXIV from *The Birds of America*
Hand-colored engraving with aquatint and etching on J. Whatman dated 1832
Plate: 19-1/4 x 12-1/8 inches (48.9 x 30.8 cm)
Sheet: 25-7/8 x 18-1/4 inches (65.7 x 46.4 cm)
Engraved, printed, and colored by R. Havell, London

Estimate: $1,000-$1,500

64024

JOHN JAMES AUDUBON (American, 1785-1851)
Children's Warbler or Yellow Warbler (Dendroica petechia)
Plate XXXV from *The Birds of America*
Hand-colored engraving with aquatint and etching on J. Whatman dated 1832
Plate: 19-3/8 x 12-1/8 inches (49.2 x 30.8 cm)
Sheet: 37-7/8 x 25-1/2 inches (96.2 x 64.8 cm)
Engraved, printed, and colored by R. Havell, London

Estimate: $1,500-$2,500

64025

JOHN JAMES AUDUBON (American, 1785-1851)
Baltimore Oriole (Icterus galbula)
Plate XII from *The Birds of America*
Hand-colored engraving with aquatint and etching on J. Whatman dated 1832
Plate: 25-1/2 x 20-1/2 inches (64.8 x 52.1 cm)
Sheet: 36-7/8 x 25-1/2 inches (93.7 x 64.8 cm)
Engraved, printed, and colored by R. Havell, London

Estimate: $3,000-$5,000

64026

JOHN JAMES AUDUBON (AMERICAN, 1785-1851)
Swamp Sparrow (Melospiza georgiana)
Plate LXIV from *The Birds of America*
Hand-colored engraving with aquatint and etching on J. Whatman dated 1832
Plate: 19-3/8 x 12-1/8 inches (49.2 x 30.8 cm)
Sheet: 37-3/4 x 25-3/8 inches (95.9 x 64.5 cm)
Engraved, printed, and colored by R. Havell, London

Estimate: $400-$600

64027

JOHN JAMES AUDUBON (American, 1785-1851)
Canadian Titmouse or Boreal Chickadee (Poecile hudsonicus), 1834
Plate CXCIV from *The Birds of America*
Hand-colored engraving with aquatint and etching on J. Whatman dated 1834
Plate: 19-1/8 x 12 inches (48.6 x 30.5 cm)
Sheet: 38-3/8 x 25-3/4 inches (97.5 x 65.4 cm)
Engraved, printed, and colored by R. Havell, London

Estimate: $2,000-$3,000

64028

JOHN JAMES AUDUBON (American, 1785-1851)
Wood Wren or House Wren (Troglodytes aedon), 1833
Plate CLXXIX from *The Birds of America*
Hand-colored engraving with aquatint and etching on J. Whatman dated 1833
Plate: 19-1/8 x 12-1/8 inches (48.6 x 30.8 cm)
Sheet: 38-1/8 x 25-3/4 inches (96.8 x 65.4 cm)
Engraved, printed, and colored by R. Havell, London

Estimate: $1,500-$2,500

64029

JOHN JAMES AUDUBON (American, 1785-1851)
Cow-pen Bird or Brown-headed Cowbird (Icterus pecoris)
Plate XCIX from *The Birds of America*
Hand-colored engraving with aquatint and etching on J. Whatman dated 1832
Plate: 12 x 19-1/4 inches (30.5 x 48.9 cm)
Sheet: 25-1/2 x 37-7/8 inches (64.8 x 96.2 cm)
Engraved, printed, and colored by R. Havell, London
Estimate: $1,200-$1,800

64030

JOHN JAMES AUDUBON (American, 1785-1851)
Brown Lark or American Pipit (Anthus rubescens)
Plate X from *The Birds of America*
Hand-colored engraving with aquatint and etching on J. Whatman dated 1832
Plate: 12-5/8 x 20-1/4 inches (32.1 x 51.4 cm)
Sheet: 25-1/2 x 37-7/8 inches (64.8 x 96.2 cm)
Engraved, printed, and colored by R. Havell, London

Estimate: $800-$1,200

64031

JOHN JAMES AUDUBON (American, 1785-1851)
Red-Breasted Nuthatch (Sitta canadensis)
Plate CV from *The Birds of America*
Hand-colored engraving with aquatint and etching on J. Whatman dated 1831
Plate: 19-1/2 x 12-1/4 inches (49.5 x 31.1 cm)
Sheet: 38-1/8 x 25-7/8 inches (96.8 x 65.7 cm)
Engraved, printed, and colored by R. Havell, London

Estimate: $800-$1,200

64032

JOHN JAMES AUDUBON (American, 1785-1851)
Brown-headed Nuthatch (Sitta pusilla)
Plate CXXV from *The Birds of America*
Hand-colored engraving with aquatint and etching on J. Whatman dated 1831
Plate: 19-5/8 x 12-1/4 inches (49.8 x 31.1 cm)
Sheet: 38-1/4 x 25-7/8 inches (97.2 x 65.7 cm)
Engraved, printed, and colored by R. Havell, London

Estimate: $800-$1,200

64033

JOHN JAMES AUDUBON (American, 1785-1851)
Red-necked Grebe (Podiceps grisegena), 1836
Plate CCXCVIII from *The Birds of America*
Hand-colored engraving with aquatint and etching on J. Whatman dated 1836
Plate: 14-3/4 x 20-3/8 inches (37.5 x 51.8 cm)
Sheet: 25-3/4 x 38-1/2 inches (65.4 x 97.8 cm)
Engraved, printed, and colored by R. Havell, London

Estimate: $1,500-$2,500

64034

JOHN JAMES AUDUBON (American, 1785-1851)
Horned Grebe (Podiceps auritus), 1835
Plate CCLIX from *The Birds of America*
Hand-colored engraving with aquatint and etching on J. Whatman dated 1835
Plate: 14-7/8 x 20-1/4 inches (37.8 x 51.4 cm)
Sheet: 26 x 38-1/2 inches (66.0 x 97.8 cm)
Engraved, printed, and colored by R. Havell, London

Estimate: $2,000-$3,000

64035

JOHN JAMES AUDUBON (American, 1785-1851)
Stormy Petrel or Wilson's Storm-Petrel (Oceanites oceanicus), 1835
Plate CCLXX from *The Birds of America*
Hand-colored engraving with aquatint and etching on J. Whatman dated 1835
Plate: 12-1/4 x 19-1/2 inches (31.1 x 49.5 cm)
Sheet: 26 x 38-1/8 inches (66.0 x 96.8 cm)
Engraved, printed, and colored by R. Havell, London

Estimate: $800-$1,200

64036

JOHN JAMES AUDUBON (American, 1785-1851)
Crested Grebe or Great Crested Grebe (Podices cristatus), 1836
Plate CCXCII from *The Birds of America*
Hand-colored engraving with aquatint and etching on J. Whatman dated 1836
Plate: 20-5/8 x 30 inches (52.4 x 76.2 cm)
Sheet: 25-7/8 x 38-1/2 inches (65.7 x 97.8 cm)
Engraved, printed, and colored by R. Havell, London

Estimate: $1,500-$2,500

64037

JOHN JAMES AUDUBON (American, 1785-1851)
Velvet Duck or White-winged Scoter (Melanitta fusca), 1835
Plate CCLXVII from *The Birds of America*
Hand-colored engraving with aquatint and etching on J. Whatman Turkey Mill dated 1835
Plate: 20-7/8 x 30-1/8 inches (53.0 x 76.5 cm)
Sheet: 25-7/8 x 37-1/2 inches (65.7 x 95.3 cm)
Engraved, printed, and colored by R. Havell, London

Estimate: $1,200-$1,500

64038

JOHN JAMES AUDUBON (American, 1785-1851)
Razor Bill (Alca torda), 1834
Plate CCXIV from *The Birds of America*
Hand-colored engraving with aquatint and etching on J. Whatman Turkey Mill dated 1834
Plate: 12-1/4 x 19-5/8 inches (31.1 x 49.8 cm)
Sheet: 25-7/8 x 38-3/8 inches (65.7 x 97.5 cm)
Engraved, printed, and colored by R. Havell, London

Estimate: $1,500-$2,500

64039

JOHN JAMES AUDUBON (American, 1785-1851)
Common Gallinule or Common Moorhen (Gallinula chloropus), 1835
Plate CCXLIV from *The Birds of America*
Hand-colored engraving with aquatint and etching on J. Whatman Turkey Mill dated 1835
Plate: 12-1/4 x 19-3/8 inches (31.1 x 49.2 cm)
Sheet: 25-7/8 x 38-3/8 inches (65.7 x 97.5 cm)
Engraved, printed, and colored by R. Havell, London

Estimate: $1,500-$2,500

64040

JOHN JAMES AUDUBON (American, 1785-1851)
Manks Shearwater or Manx Shearwater (Puffinus puffinus), 1836
Plate CCXCV from *The Birds of America*
Hand-colored engraving with aquatint and etching on J. Whatman dated 1836
Plate: 16-1/4 x 21-5/8 inches (41.3 x 54.9 cm)
Sheet: 25-7/8 x 38-1/2 inches (65.7 x 97.8 cm)
Engraved, printed, and colored by R. Havell, London

Estimate: $3,000-$5,000

64041

JOHN JAMES AUDUBON (American, 1785-1851)
Pectoral Sandpiper (Calidris melanotos)
Plate CCXCIV from *The Birds of America*, 1836
Hand-colored engraving with aquatint and etching on J. Whatman dated 1836
Plate: 12-1/8 x 19-3/8 inches (30.8 x 49.2 cm)
Sheet: 25-3/4 x 38-1/2 inches (65.4 x 97.8 cm)
Engraved, printed, and colored by R. Havell, London

Estimate: $2,000-$3,000

64042

JOHN JAMES AUDUBON (American, 1785-1851)
Purple Sandpiper (Calidris maritima), 1835
Plate CCLXXXIV from *The Birds of America*
Hand-colored engraving with aquatint and etching on J. Whatman dated 1836
Plate: 12-3/8 x 19-3/4 inches (31.4 x 50.2 cm)
Sheet: 25-7/8 x 38-1/2 inches (65.7 x 97.8 cm)
Engraved, printed, and colored by R. Havell, London

Estimate: $2,000-$3,000

64043

JOHN JAMES AUDUBON (American, 1785-1851)
Buff Breasted Sandpiper (Tryngites subruficollis), 1835
Plate CCLXV from *The Birds of America*
Hand-colored engraving with aquatint and etching on J. Whatman dated 1835
Plate: 12-1/4 x 19-1/2 inches (31.1 x 49.5 cm)
Sheet: 25-7/8 x 38-1/2 inches (65.7 x 97.8 cm)
Engraved, printed, and colored by R. Havell, London

Estimate: $4,000-$6,000

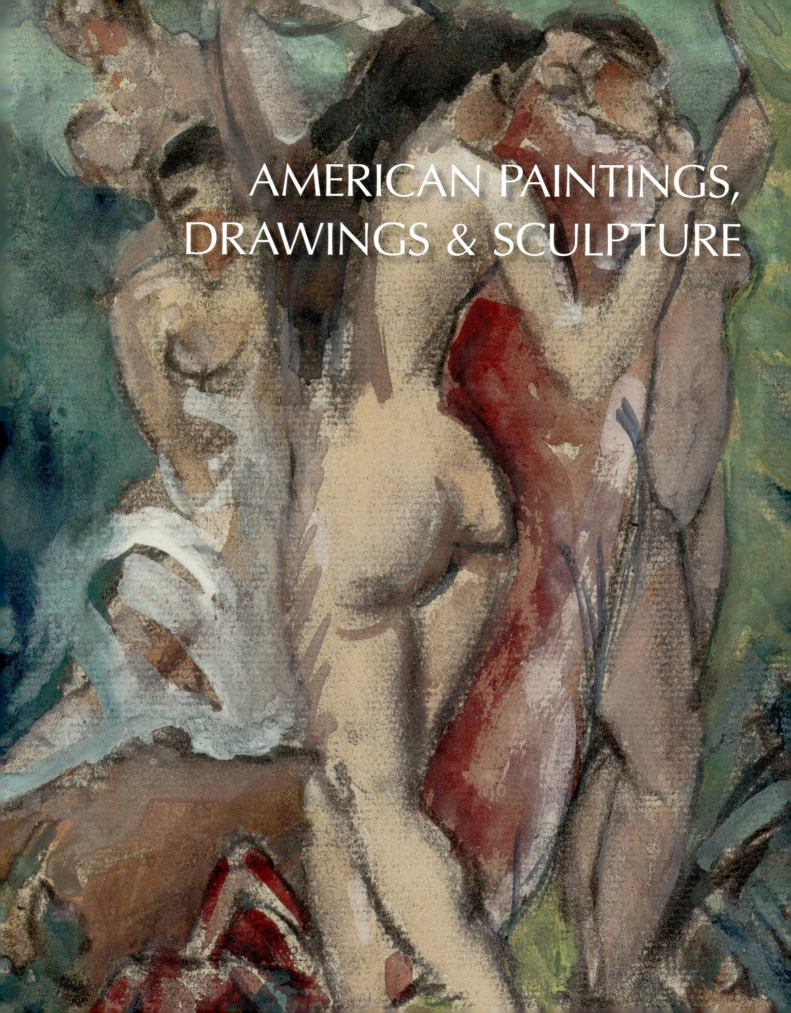

AMERICAN PAINTINGS, DRAWINGS & SCULPTURE

64044

ROBERT HENRI (American, 1865-1929)
Lucinda, Mexican Girl, 1916
Oil on canvas
24 x 20 inches (61.0 x 50.8 cm)
Signed lower left: *Robert Henri*

PROVENANCE:
Mr. Philip M. Sharples, West Chester, Pennsylvania, 1917;
By descent to the present owner.

EXHIBITED:
Chicago Arts Club, Chicago, Illinois, 1916;
The Pennsylvania Academy of the Fine Arts, Philadelphia, Pennsylvania, "One Hundred and Twelfth Annual Exhibition," 1917 (label verso).

We wish to thank Dr. Valerie Ann Leeds for her gracious assistance in cataloguing this painting, listed in the record book as no. J 244.

Estimate: $400,000-$600,000

The people I like to paint are "my people," whoever they may be, wherever they may exist, the people through whom dignity of life is manifest, that is, who are in some way expressing themselves naturally along the lines nature intended for them.[1]

In 1916 when Robert Henri painted this fetching portrait, *Lucinda, Mexican Girl*, he was at the height of his success, wearing several large hats: he was an outstanding teacher at the New York School of Art and the "Manet of Manhattan," so nicknamed for his realist, sensitive portraits executed with vigorous brushwork and spontaneity. Portraiture was Henri's true calling, and he wrote and lectured extensively about identifying ideal subjects, what he termed "his people," whose outward expressions and demeanor connoted inner strength and spirituality. Although Henri found many of "his people" in New York, he traveled actively throughout the United States and Europe in search of distinctive ethnic types. It was on one of these early trips to Southern California in 1914 that Henri first painted Hispanic and Native American sitters, finding in them exotic beauty and stately character.

I was not interested in these people to sentimentalize over them. . . . I am looking at each individual with the eager hope of finding there something of the dignity of life. . . . I do not wish to explain these people. I do not wish to preach through them, I only want to find whatever of the great spirit there is in the Southwest. If I can hold it on my canvas I am satisfied.[2]

During this same trip to San Diego in 1914, Henri met the catalyst for his most important series of Southwestern paintings, Dr. Edgar L. Hewett, Director of both the School of American Archaeology and the Museum of New Mexico in Santa Fe. Dr. Hewett urged Henri to come experience Santa Fe and offered him the use of a downtown studio in the old Palace of the Governors. From July through October 1916, Henri and his wife, Marjorie, settled there and, with Dr. Hewett, met local Indians, attended ceremonial dances at Taos and Acoma, and visited the Taos and Laguna pueblos. Santa Fe, with its light-filled landscapes and colorful native populations, quickly became one of Henri's favorite homes away from home. He made three working trips there, in 1916, 1917, and 1922, producing around 245 paintings, mostly portraits, of exceptional and original quality. Indeed, this Santa Fe period was unquestionably one of the strongest in his career.

I have never respected any man more than I have some children. In the faces of children I have seen a look of wisdom . . . with . . . such certainty that I knew it . . . was the expression of a whole race.[3]

The great majority of Henri's Santa Fe portraits focus on Hispanic and Native American children and teenagers, in whom he saw especial dignity and vitality. Unlike his hallmark Ashcan School portraits of children, which feature dark, Old Master-inspired palettes and simple backdrops, the Santa Fe portraits exhibit vibrant coloration and ethnic costumes and accessories, such as blankets, jewelry, and pottery. Henri painted many of his young models numerous times — Gregorita, ten portraits; Juanita, ten; Tilly, eleven; and Francisco, four — and some of them on multiple trips to Santa Fe — Julianita, six portraits in 1917 and four in 1922. By far, his most imaged, and thus likely his most beloved, model was Lucinda, a six-year-old Mexican girl, whom he painted twenty-two times, ten in 1916 and twelve in 1917. The current lot, *Lucinda, Mexican Girl* from 1916, is a superior example. As in others from the Lucinda series, Henri depicts the girl in native costume with loose pigtails and full lips, and he suggests a geometric ethnic textile for the backdrop (much like the Native American blankets that offset his Indian subjects). In some of her portraits, Lucinda appears more demure and pensive, her head turned aside and her eyes averted. Yet, here, she is audacious, almost defiant, as she stares directly at the viewer and crosses her arms. Henri hinted at Lucinda's strong personality in a letter from 1917: "Lucinda is a fine little saffron colored queen of about six years. Last year she was not an enthusiast about posing but this year she likes to come."[4]

I believe that great pictures can be painted with the use of most pure colors, and that these colors can be so transformed to our vision that they will seem to have gradations which do not actually exist in them. This will be brought about by a science of juxtaposition and an employment of areas that will be extraordinary.[5]

(continued on pg. 82)

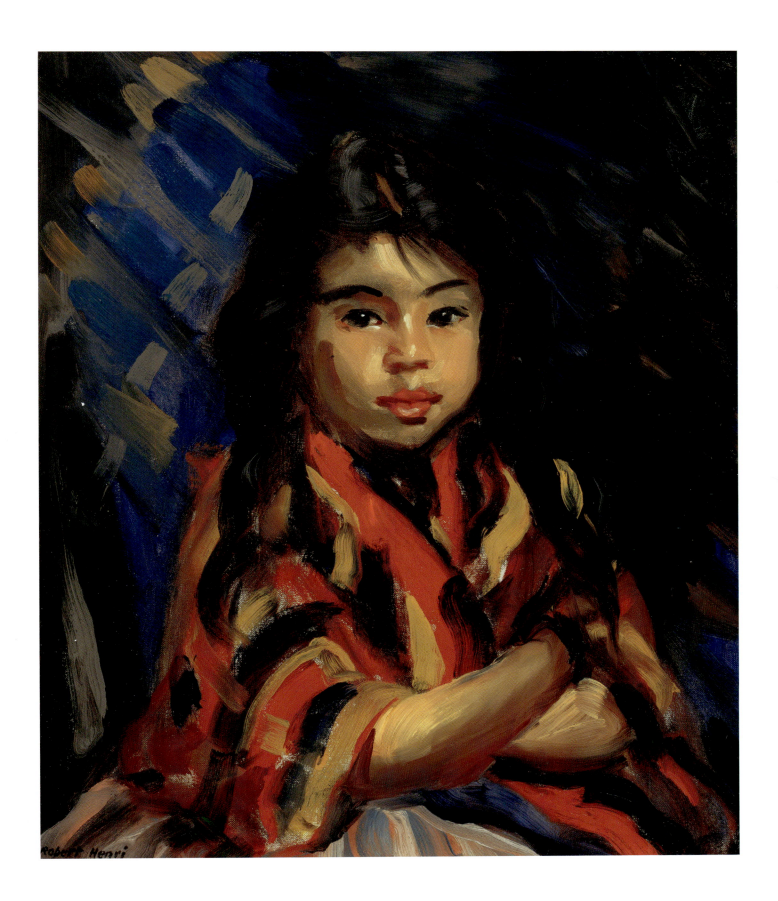

Gesture expresses through form and color the states of life. Work with great speed. . . . Finish as quickly as you can. There is no virtue in delaying. Get the greatest possibility of expression in the larger masses first. . . . Do it all in one sitting if you can. In one minute if you can. . . . The most vital things in the look of a face. . . endure only for a moment.[6]

In *Lucinda, Mexican Girl*, Henri brilliantly underscores the strong-willed disposition of the sitter through bold color and energized brushwork. Since 1909, he had been practicing Hardesty Maratta's color theory, which organized colors, like musical notes, in chords, or triads. Henri's early portraits exhibit simplified, tonal palettes injected with an occasional primary color. Yet Santa Fe brought out a new vibrancy in his palette, exemplified here in the principal triad of bright orange-red, yellow-orange, and blue. The cool blue of the background cloth dynamically juxtaposes the warm orange-reds and yellows of Lucinda's striped Mexican shawl, forcing the eye to seek relief in the earth tones of her face. Like these pulsing hues, the gestural brushstrokes — the vertical stripes of the shawl and the diagonal lines of the background cloth — direct attention to her visage at the center of the composition. For Henri, the more spontaneous and gestural the brushwork, the likelier he was to capture the fleeting essence of the sitter's expression and inner spirit. The brushwork in *Lucinda, Mexican Girl*, a true tour de force in its movement, impasto, and sheen, appears so freshly executed that the paint could almost be drying — and viewers almost meeting Lucinda in the flesh.

I advise you to enjoy every minute you have left of beautiful Santa Fe and make up your mind that while you will come bodily to New York, you will remain in the spiritual remoteness and aloofness which may be possible in Santa Fe.[7]

Henri's positive experience in Santa Fe impacted other artists, as well as the broader New Mexico community. Thanks to his encouragement, artists from his New York circle came to Santa Fe: George Bellows; Leon Kroll; John Sloan, who spent one season there for the next thirty years; and Randall Davey, who ultimately settled just outside of the town. Henri also worked with Dr. Hewett and the Santa Fe Museum to establish more democratic exhibition policies for contemporary artists. Most significant, Santa Fe left a lasting imprint on Henri himself. As the art historian Valerie Ann Leeds writes, "Henri never again attained the fresh originality of the 1916 and 1917 Santa Fe portraits. Santa Fe, therefore, represents the last important phase in the development of his portraiture."[8]

1:R. Henri, *The Art Spirit*, New York, 1951, p. 107.
2:Ibid., p. 112.
3:V. Leeds, *Robert Henri in Santa Fe: His Work and Influence*, Santa Fe, 1998, p. 14.
4:Ibid., p. 17.
5:Henri, p. 41.
6:Ibid., p. 10-11.
7:Leeds, pp. 26-7. From a 1920 letter from Henri to fellow artist John Sloan.
8:Ibid., p. 36.

64045
GASTON LACHAISE (French/American, 1882-1935)
Bust of Woman (Garden Figure) (LF 175B)
Bronze with brown patina
28-1/2 inches (72.4 cm) high
Inscribed on verso along edge of woman's back: *LACHAISE ESTATE 2/12*
Stamped on verso along lower edge: *Modern Art Foundry cachet and casting date (92)*

PROVENANCE:
Lachaise Foundation, Boston, Massachusetts, 1992;
[With]Salander-O'Reilley, New York, 1993-98;
Private collection, New York, acquired from the above, 1998;
Private collection, Oyster Bay, New York, by descent from the above.

LITERATURE:
D. B. Goodall, "Gaston Lachaise, Sculptor," Ph.D. dissertation, Harvard University, Cambridge, Massachusetts, 1969, vol. 2, p. 449 (plaster model for *Bust of Woman [Garden Figure]*);
Salander O'Reilly Galleries, Inc. *Gaston Lachaise: Sculpture*, exhibition catalogue, New York, 1991, pp. 77, 84, no. 34 (another example illustrated);
Galerie Gerald Piltzer, *Gaston Lachaise: Sculptures*, exhibition catalogue, Paris, 1992, pp. 24, 60, no. 24 (another example illustrated);
S. Hunter, *Lachaise*, New York 1993, pp. 206-08, 245 (another example illustrated);
Philip and Muriel Berman Museum of Art at Ursinus College, *Ten Years of Collecting: The Permanent Collection in Context*, exhibition catalogue, Collegeville, Pennsylvania, 1999, p. 20, 29 (another example illustrated);

We are grateful to the art historian Virginia Budny for her gracious assistance in cataloguing this lot.

Estimate: $15,000-$20,000

According to Virginia Budny, Gaston Lachaise's *Bust of Woman (Garden Figure)* (Lachaise Foundation no. 175B) was derived from a monumental garden sculpture of a standing nude woman commissioned from him by Nelson A. Rockefeller in April 1935. Lachaise's full-size model for Rockefeller's statue (LF 175) was completed and cast in cement during the next five weeks; the statue is now owned by the Hood Museum of Art, Dartmouth College, Hanover, New Hampshire. (Four other examples of the statue were also produced in cement, three of which are owned by the Portland Museum of Art, Portland, Maine; the Smith College Museum of Art, Northampton, Massachusetts; and the Bayly Art Museum of the University of Virginia, Charlottesville.) The statue, which evokes a mood of serenity and abundance, was directly inspired by Isabel Nagle (1872-1957), Lachaise's beloved wife and muse. In June — nine months before Lachaise's unexpected death — Rockefeller commissioned a bronze cast of the statue's head. This bronze (LF 175A), completed by the following September, is unlocated. It had been made from part of a two-piece plaster of the head and upper torso of *Woman (Garden Figure)* (LF 175B). During the same period, Lachaise reworked a plaster cast of *Woman (Garden Figure)* (LF 175) to create a second, unidealized version of the statue; this version (LF 137) was first issued in bronze in about 1973 for the Lachaise Foundation, which oversees the sculptor's estate.

In 1991, the Foundation authorized the first of a projected edition of twelve bronze casts to be made from Lachaise's two-piece plaster of the head and upper torso of *Woman (Garden Figure)* (LF 175B). The second bronze in this series, the present example, was cast in the following year. The third bronze — the last in the edition to have been produced thus far — is owned by the Philip and Muriel Berman Museum of Art at Ursinus College, Collegeville, Pennsylvania. Lachaise's plaster model of *Bust of Woman (Garden Figure)* belongs to the Lachaise Foundation.

This particular lot is accompanied by a white wooden pedestal measuring 43.5 x 32 x 17 inches.

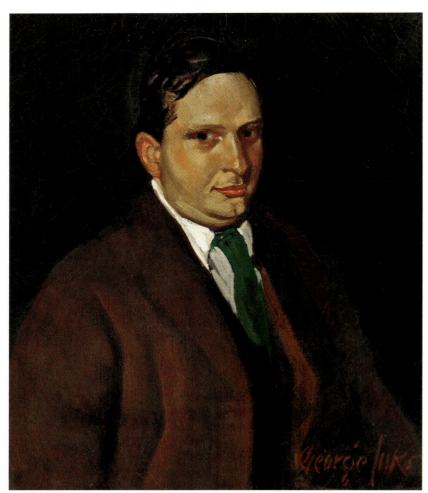

64046

GEORGE BENJAMIN LUKS (American, 1867-1933)
The Green Tie (Portrait of Edward H. Smith), circa 1915
Oil on canvas
30 x 25 inches (76.2 x 63.5 cm)
Signed lower right: *George Luks*

PROVENANCE:
Berry-Hill Galleries, New York (label verso);
Private collection, 1978;
Sotheby's, New York, *American Paintings, Drawings and Sculpture Including*
Property from the John F. Eulich Collection, May 20, 1998, lot 38.

EXHIBITED:
Berry-Hill Galleries, New York, "Continuities: American Figure Painting 1900-1950",
October 11-November 5, 1983, no. 18 (label verso).

Edward H. Smith (1882-1927) was a journalist, editor, writer and a close friend of the artist.

Estimate: $4,000-$6,000

64047

MAX KALISH (American, 1891-1945)
The Structural Steel Worker, 1926
Bronze with brown patina
18-3/4 inches (47.6 cm) high on a 3/4 inches high marble base
Inscribed on the base: *M. Kalish 26*
Stamped along the base: *MERONI RADICE / CIRE / PERDUE / PARIS*

PROPERTY FROM A PROMINENT CLEVELAND, OHIO FAMILY

PROVENANCE:
(Possibly) Korner and Wood, Cleveland, Ohio, *circa* 1926-27;
William R. Hopkins (1869-1961), noted Cleveland, Ohio politician and industrialist, until 1961;
David J. Hopkins, Esq., nephew of the above, Cleveland, Ohio, by descent, 1961 until circa 1980-82;
Thence by descent in the family.

LITERATURE (various casts):
"Walt Whitman of Sculpture," *New York Post*, November 19, 1926;
New York Herald Tribune, review of Kalish exhibition at Feragil Galleries, New York, November 28, 1926;
"Apollo of the Sky-Scrapers," *The Literary Digest*, December 18, 1926;
The Plain Dealer, review of Kalish exhibition at Korner and Wood, Cleveland, Ohio, December 5, 1926;
Detroit News, review of Kalish exhibition at Hanna-Thompson Galleries, Detroit, Michigan, January 16, 1927;
N. Lawson Lewis, *The Sculpture of Max Kalish*, Cleveland, Ohio, 1933, n.p., pl. 30;
E. Genauer, *Labor Sculpture by Max Kalish*, New York, 1938, n.p., pl. 29.

Estimate: $15,000-$25,000

During the early months of 1926, the Polish-born American sculptor Max Kalish was in Paris bringing to fruition a body of work that would eventually secure his reputation as one of the most important American sculptors of his time—a series of bronze laborers. Most of the figures were associated with the steel industry and steel construction work, and the artist's specific models for these sculptures were Clevelanders. Kalish drafted them personally from the American Steel and Wire Company (*Cleveland News*, November 20, 1927) to pose for him, so that the physiques depicted in his sculptures were in every way appropriate to the tasks being portrayed. After creating original circa 18-inch models of his riveter, structural steel worker, lineman, sledge driver and other workers in Cleveland, Kalish transported them to Paris to be cast into bronze at the expert foundry, Meroni Radice. He then shipped the bronzes back to the United States for exhibition in late 1926. The laborers were first shown in Cleveland at Kalish's dealer, Korner and Wood Gallery on Euclid Boulevard, before embarking on a multi-city tour to major industrial metropolises including Detroit and New York.

The reviews of the 1926 and 1927 exhibits of Kalish's laborers were almost universally positive, celebrating the artist's treatment of a very American subject in a medium long cherished by European artists. As a major steel producer, Cleveland (and its art critics) particularly appreciated Kalish's realism, and noted more than once that that the artist's own experience as an industrial worker accounts for the truth in the portrayal of his subject. Emily Genauer echoed this idea in 1938, writing, "He is qualified to speak as he does of the movements and rhythms of laborers. He has himself, in the past, been one of them, working in his youth as "a hand" in Cleveland machine shops. He has labored alongside the great, muscular figures he portrays, the bull-necked, powerful, heavy-footed steelworkers, linemen and sledge drivers."

Despite the elegance of the pose of Kalish's *Structural Steel Worker*, "swinging high on beams above a churning city," Kalish was quick to point out that his laborers are not "propaganda pieces at all, [not] polemics against the abuses of exploitation of labor," nor the deification of it. His intent was, rather, to show in his art a dominant American type, and the natural beauty of that form which, as Kalish described it, "is expressive of poised power held in check."

The first owner of this bronze was William R. Hopkins, who served as Cleveland's first City Manager from 1924-29, was responsible for building the old Cleveland Stadium and Cleveland Municipal Airport (now named Cleveland Hopkins International Airport in his honor), and implemented the building of the Terminal Tower and the creation of the Cleveland Cultural Gardens.

64048
GUY PÈNE DU BOIS (American, 1884-1958)
Girl in Striped Sweater, circa 1938
Oil on canvas
36 x 29 inches (91.4 x 73.7 cm)
Signed and dated lower left: *Guy Pène du Bois 38*

PROVENANCE:
James Graham & Sons, New York.

In 1930, following the crash of the New York stock market, the art critic and social realist painter Guy Pène du Bois reluctantly returned to America after nearly a decade in Paris. Abroad, Pène du Bois had developed his mature figurative aesthetic: stylized and impassive characters placed in fashionable settings, which recall images from *Vanity Fair* and the *New Yorker* and evoke the shallow beauty of the Roaring Twenties. Now back in New York, he continued to explore subjects that had interested him in Paris, in particular, café denizens and circus or carnival entertainers, yet the tone of these works is more mysterious and less humorous. For example, in *Trapeze Performers* (1931) and *Carnival Interlude* (1935), mannequin-like female figures exude psychological alienation amidst their audiences.

Eager to make money during the 1930s, Pène du Bois taught at the Art Students League, accepted WPA mural commissions, and began painting more portraits, many of women posed in chairs. Unlike his earlier caricature-like portraits, these works exhibit more sculptural forms, brighter colors, and loose brushwork, while maintaining an air of dramatic tension.

The present lot, *Girl in Striped Sweater*, exemplifies Pène du Bois' monumental portraits of pensive women from this period. Like *Portrait of a Woman* (1932), *Meditation* (1936), and *Yvonne in a Purple Coat* (1938), *Girl in Striped Sweater* angles the sitter away from the viewer, her gaze lost in reverie. Her slightly awkward features - distant expression, hefty chest, elongated arms, and blue skirt that ambiguously blends into the background and the chair arm - conjure up an enthroned Mannerist Madonna. Pène du Bois also references his own cafe and carnival paintings through the object of the red striped sweater, which he makes a focal point of the painting; indeed, this same red striped pattern appears on the shorts of the central female acrobat in *Carnival Interlude* and on the shirt of a model in his 1937 *Girls Against the Sky*. With its graphic patterning, expressive color and brushwork, and theme of introspection, *Girl in Striped Sweater* perfectly illustrates modernist figure painting. Inviting interpretation on the part of the viewer, it remains one of Pène du Bois's most haunting portraits.

Estimate: $20,000-$30,000

64049

EVERETT SHINN (American, 1876-1953)
Two Girls Dressing for a Party, 1914
Pastel and gouache on paper
29 x 27 inches (73.7 x 68.6 cm) (sight)
Signed and dated lower center: *Everett Shinn 1914*

PROPERTY FROM A DISTINGUISHED PRIVATE COLLECTOR

PROVENANCE:
Sotheby's, New York, December 6, 1984, lot 182;
Acquired by the present owner from the above.

It is seemingly incongruous that Everett Shinn, noted imager of New York's high society as seen in *Two Girls Dressing for a Party*, had first established himself as an illustrator of gritty urban streetscapes. Born in New Jersey, Shinn trained at the Pennsylvania Academy of the Fine Arts before taking a job in the art department of the *Philadelphia Press* in 1893. Here, he met colleagues George Luks, William Glackens, and John Sloan, and together, after moving to New York in the late 1890s, they later formed the "Eight," an anti-academic, social realist group under the leadership of portraitist Robert Henri. Shinn's job as an artist-reporter for the *New York Herald* informed his early, unidealized subjects, both working-class spaces - pool halls, saloons, and tenements - and downtown spectacles — fire engines racing to the rescue, ship workers brawling on docks, ragpickers trudging through the snow, and poor families being evicted from their homes.

Shinn's illustration background also influenced his style. In an effort to evoke newspaper drama and the quick, immediate sketch of a reporter on the beat, he utilized exaggerated, diagonal lines and plunging perspectives, and he commonly situated the viewer in the midst of the action. Too, Shinn favored pastel over oil for many of his street scenes, as it allowed him to achieve atmospheric effects, graphic contrasts, and vigorous lines. Critics and gallery audiences marveled over the unconventionally large scale of Shinn's "urban pastels," as well as their masterful technique: he would first blend colored pastels into wet paper, thereby creating a lush, gouache-like density, then detail his forms with energized lines of ink, charcoal, or white pastel.

By the 1910s, Shinn was still experimenting with pastel, but he had shifted his focus from downtown to uptown subjects, such as theater performers and fashionable society. Patrons like the architect Stanford White and the actress Elsie de Wolfe helped him secure commissions to paint set decorations for theaters and Rococo-style murals for fancy apartments. Shinn's images of beautifully costumed singers, dancers, and actresses on stage and of ladies dressing in their boudoirs borrowed directly from the Impressionist aesthetic of painter-pastelist Edgar Degas.

The present *Two Girls Dressing for a Party* exemplifies Shinn's Degas-inspired depictions of performers. Here, in one of his large-scale pastels, Shinn highlights not merely the charming sisters, but their gorgeous fabrics: ruffled white dresses, giant taffeta bows, and corresponding pink-and-blue silk throws (or robes) draped over chairs. Like Shinn's stage actresses, the girls prance into the spotlight, yet they do so within the intimate, protected confines of an upper-class sitting room. His trademark diagonal lines, angular forms, and tumbling perspective activate the composition and pull the viewer into this upscale urban "drama."

Estimate: $30,000-$50,000

64050
EDWARD HENRY POTTHAST (American, 1857-1927)
A Summer Vacation
Oil on canvas
16 x 20 inches (40.6 x 50.8 cm)
Signed lower left: *E. Potthast*
Artist's label verso

PROVENANCE:
Chapellier Galleries, New York (label verso);
Sotheby's, New York, *American Paintings, Drawings and Sculpture Including Property from the John F. Eulich Collection*, May 20, 1998, lot 30;
John H. Surovek Gallery, Palm Beach, Florida;
Private collection, Maryland.

At the turn of the twentieth century, city living meant overcrowded tenements, shantytowns, grime and poverty for many New York City residents. But when weekends came around, sorrows were put on hold as masses of working-class men, women and children flocked to the nearby beaches. In *A Summer Vacation* Edward Henry Potthast masterfully captures the blissful spirit of seaside holidays with his depiction of a couple relaxing in the sand along the seashore. The artist presents this moment in time with a flourish of brushwork and high-keyed colors that capture the essence of the day.

Potthast was born in Cincinnati, Ohio, at a time when the city was a burgeoning art center in the Midwest. In 1869, at the age of twelve, he became a charter student at Cincinnati's new McMicken School of Design and studied there for over a decade. Like many American artists, Potthast also traveled extensively to further his career. In 1882, he spent time in Munich, Antwerp and Paris. Through the Munich School's bold style of depicting tone and atmosphere, Potthast learned to work vigorously with paint applied directly onto the canvas, and to increase his sensitivity to form. The Barbizon painters influenced Potthast's interest in everyday life in contrast to the heroic or idealized subject common in his day. Yet it was Potthast's 1889 trip to the artist's colony of Grèz-sur-Loing, France, which was undoubtedly the most influential in the development of his *oeuvre*. "When in Grèz," notes Dr. William Gerdts, "Potthast 'fell under the influence of [Robert] Vonnoh and [Roderick] O'Connor [sic] and became a convert to the new school of Impressionism.' The results of Potthast's conversion to the new aesthetic were immediate, and were seen in the work Potthast brought back with him to his native town. He continued to paint with the bravura brushwork and colorism of Impressionism after he moved to New York in 1896, and it continued when he began to specialize in scenes of children and other bathers at Brooklyn beaches...which then became his specialty after 1910."[1]

By the 1910s, Potthast established his studio on West 59th Street in New York City, in proximity to the crowded resorts of Brighton Beach and Coney Island. The seashore lent itself to a bold Impressionist treatment; Potthast captured the motion of the surf, children playing, and the casual poses of people at leisure called for Potthast's quick, animated style. In one of the most effervescent and successful of these compositions, *A Summer Vacation*, Potthast uses a high horizon line to accentuate the bustle and liveliness of the many city-folk enjoying a day at the beach. The composition is filled with colorfully dressed women and children. These dashes of interlocking colors and forms typify the artist's creative, Impressionist style through the use of broad and direct brushwork.

All of Potthast's artistic devices come together in *A Summer Vacation* to form a highly successful composition. J.W. Young, a long-time friend of the artist and Chicago art dealer, commented in 1920: "Potthast has found his greatest pleasure painting the happy groups which crowd the beaches near New York...Potthast does not paint individuals on the sands. He interprets the joy of folks on a care-free day. Whenever any artist does some one thing better than it has been done before, distinction is sure to come to him sooner or later. But when he does something that strikes the finest chord in human nature better than anyone else has done it, fame will mark that artist as one of her own."[2] *A Summer Afternoon* is a classic example of Potthast's spontaneous painting style. The painting's quick brush strokes and vibrant palette perfectly encapsulate the essence of carefree leisure.

1: *Lasting Impressions: American Painters in France 1865-1915*, Evanston, Illinois, 1992, p. 67
2: as quoted in Ran Gallery, *Edward Henry Potthast: An American Painter*, exhibition catalogue, Cincinnati, Ohio, 1994, p. 15

Estimate: $150,000-$200,000

64051

CHILDE HASSAM (American, 1859-1935)
Perros-Guirec, Côtes du Nord, France, 1910
Oil on panel
7 x 10 inches (17.8 x 25.4 cm)
Signed and dated lower right: *Childe Hassam / 1910*
Inscribed with artist's device verso

PROPERTY FROM A DISTINGUISHED PRIVATE COLLECTOR

PROVENANCE:
The artist;
American Academy of Arts and Letters, New York, bequest from the above, 1935;
[With] Milch Galleries, New York, 1944;
(Possibly) Parke Bernet, New York, March 31, 1949, lot 127 (as *Perreos (Cotes Du Nord) Near Brest*);
Private collection, circa 1950s;
By descent:
Private collector, Connecticut.

EXHIBITED:
(Possibly) Macbeth Galleries, New York, "Second Exhibition of Intimate Paintings," December 1918, no. 37 (as *Beach in France*).

This work will be included in Stuart P. Feld's and Kathleen M. Burnside's forthcoming *catalogue raisonné* of the artist's work.

During the summer of 1910, after selling four major paintings to an Oregon collector, the American Impressionist Childe Hassam had sufficient funds to return to Europe after a fourteen-year hiatus. From London, Hassam and his wife ventured to Paris, yet finding the July heat and crowds in the city oppressive, they traveled to picturesque towns along the northwest coast of France, including Lannion, Nemours, Grez-Sur-Long, and Perros-Guirec.

Painted during this vacation, *Perros-Guirec, Côtes du Nord, France* beautifully synthesizes the Impressionist technique that Hassam had developed on his first trip to Paris during the 1880s with a newer Post-Impressionist handling of forms and space. As in his earlier Impressionist landscapes, Hassam employs both dazzling sunlight and jewel-toned colors to enliven the composition: a swath of coastline dotted with bathers and cabanas at the foot of the town's verdant, rolling hills. Hassam's Impressionist brushwork – for example, the vertical flecks representing people and buildings, the horizontal strokes of white sand, and the diagonal hatch marks of the foreground foliage -- further energize an otherwise placid setting. However, Hassam's simplification of forms and his distinctive ordering of space into flattened fields of color – turquoise sky and waves, azure water, pink beach, and emerald- and blue-green hills – point to Post-Impressionist influences on his work. Indeed, it is likely that he had studied paintings by the Post-Impressionists Edouard Vuillard and Pierre Bonnard while in Paris, only months earlier. In *Perros-Guirec, Côtes du Nord, France*, Hassam tips his hat to vanguard French art, while superbly demonstrating his mature aesthetic.

Estimate: $100,000-$150,000

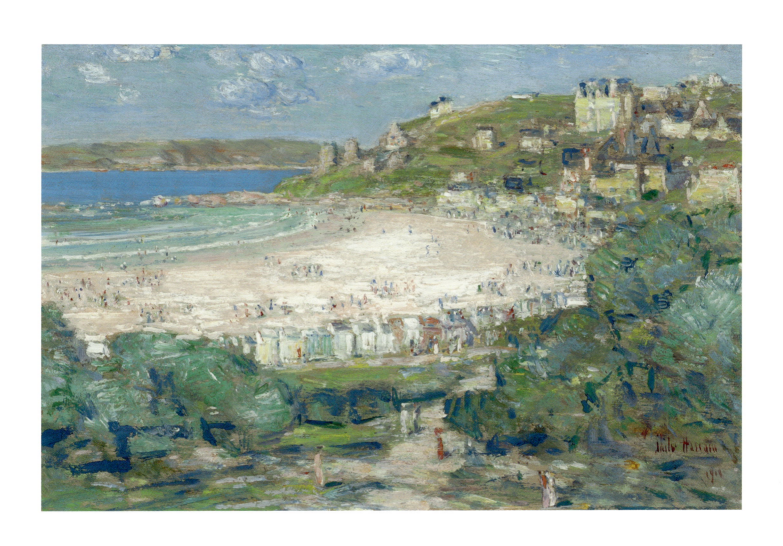

64052

ERNEST MARTIN HENNINGS (American, 1886-1956)
Idle Gondolas, Venice, Italy
Oil on canvasboard
14 x 14 inches (35.6 x 35.6 cm)
Signed lower right: *E.M. Hennings*

PROVENANCE:
Chicago Galleries Association, Chicago, Illinois, *circa* 1954;
Zaplin Lampert Gallery, Santa Fe, New Mexico (labels verso).

Estimate: $6,000-$8,000

64053

THEODORE EARL BUTLER (American, 1861-1936)
Fireworks, Bridge at Vernon, France, circa 1908
Gouache on paper
15-1/2 x 18-3/8 inches (39.4 x 46.7 cm) (sheet)
Signed lower left: *T.E. Butler*

PROPERTY FROM A DISTINGUISHED PRIVATE COLLECTOR

PROVENANCE:
[With]Hutton Galleries, New York;
Private collection, Arkansas;
[With]Davis Auction Galleries, New York;
Private collection, Atlanta, Georgia, acquired from the above, 1992;
Spanierman Galleries, New York (label verso);
Acquired by the present owner from the above, 2009.

RELATED LITERATURE:
R.H. Love, *Theodore Earl Butler: Emergence from Monet's Shadow*, Chicago, Illinois, 1985, p. 259, pl. 62.
Maxwell Galleries, *Theodore Earl Butler: American Impressionist*, exhibition catalogue, San Francisco, California, 1972, pp. 26-7, pl. 591, 592, and 676.

This work will be included in the forthcoming *catalogue raisonn*é being compiled by Patrick Bertrand.

Estimate: $25,000-$35,000

64054

FREDERICK CARL FRIESEKE (American, 1874-1939)
On the Beach (Girl in Blue), 1913
Oil on canvas
32 x 32 inches (81.3 x 81.3 cm)
Signed lower right: *F.C. Frieseke*

PROVENANCE:
Collection of Josephine Pettengill Everett (Mrs. Henry A. Everett), Cleveland, Ohio, and Pasadena, California;
Pasadena Art Institute, Josephine P. Everett Collection, Pasadena, California;
The Cleveland Museum of Art, Cleveland, Ohio, 1946;
Vose Galleries LLC, Boston, Massachusetts (labels verso);
Valley House Gallery, Dallas;
Private collection, Dallas, acquired from the above, 1965.

EXHIBITED:
Salon de la Société Nationale des Beaux-Arts, Paris, France, 1913, no. 481 or 484;
University of New Mexico Art Gallery, Albuquerque, New Mexico, and elsewhere, "Impressionism in America," February-March, 1965, no. 11;
The Telfair Academy of Arts and Sciences, Savannah, Georgia, and elsewhere, "Frederick Frieseke, 1874-1939," November-December 1974, p. 16-17, no. 8, as *Girl in Blue*;
Hirschl & Adler Galleries, New York, "Frieseke Retrospective Exhibition," 1975;
Berry-Hill Galleries, New York, "Frederick C. Frieseke: Women in Repose," May 2-June 23, 1990, no. 10, (label verso).

LITERATURE:
"A Summer's Day," LIFE Magazine, July 23, 1965, pp. 76-7, illustrated as *Girl in Blue*.

This painting will be included in the forthcoming *catalogue raisonné* of Frieseke's work being compiled by Nicholas Kilmer, the artist's grandson, and sponsored by Hollis Taggart Galleries, New York.

Estimate: $600,000-$800,000

Frederick Frieseke's exquisite *On the Beach* may be set on the island of Corsica, yet its technique and subject ultimately stem from his experience at the artist colony in Giverny in northern France. Lured from Paris in 1906 by his fellow American expatriate friends Frederick MacMonnies and Stanton Young, Frieseke and his new bride, Sadie, moved to Giverny, the site of Claude Monet's famous house and gardens around which an Impressionist art colony had been growing for two decades. The culture of Giverny was decidedly leisured and bucolic: the Friesekes played tennis, took tea, boated, strolled along country paths, and attended music parties with a whole host of American artists, including the Ernest Blumenscheins, Theodore Butler, the Karl Buehrs, the Henry Hubells, Lawton Parker, and the Guy Roses. Captivated by Monet's gardens, Frederick and Sadie also spent time shaping their own a sumptuous garden, which they organized by color and texture in order to inspire Frieseke's paintings; here, carefully placed green lawn furniture, complementing their yellow house, welcomed guests and models alike.

In this artistic Giverny environment, two major shifts occurred in Frieseke's work: first, he abandoned the tonal "color fields" of his Whistler-esque Paris paintings, in favor of a more vivid Impressionist palette and broken brushwork. Second, he began painting *en plein air*, experimenting with the effects of sunlight on his female models, both clothed and unclothed, whom he placed in gardens, on riverbanks, and in boats. Frieseke elaborated on the importance of outdoor light in a 1914 interview: "It is sunshine, flowers in sunshine; girls in sunshine; the nude in sunshine, which I have been principally interested in for eight years. . . ."[1]

(fig. 1) *On the Dunes*, 1913, oil on canvas, 32 x 26 in.

In search of sunlight after an especially rainy summer of 1912, Frederick, Sadie, and his favorite model, Marcelle, spent the next winter in Corsica, a popular Mediterranean retreat for French high society. Over the next several months, Frieseke produced three major paintings of Marcelle, including the present *On the Beach*, all of which were exhibited in the 1913 Salon of the Société Nationale des Beaux-Arts in Paris. The most elegant and compositionally sophisticated of the six, *On the Beach* depicts Marcelle as if straight off the pages of *Gazette du Bon Ton*, wearing fashionable resort wear: ankle-laced slippers, form-fitting dress with ruffle trim, and feathered cap. Her Japanese parasol, prominent in numerous of Frieseke's Giverny paintings, serves as both a decorative accessory and a practical sunshade. Frieseke also painted Marcelle nude on the beach, a practice that would have been unthinkable in the United States in 1913. In the related *On the Dunes* (fig. 1), Marcelle appears seemingly moments after her stroll in *On the Beach*: superimposed upon a backdrop of dune grasses, she now kneels completely naked on a white cloth (draped over the stool in *On the Beach*) and on her blue dress that she has just removed, with the parasol neatly folded by her side. Nicholas Kilmer, grandson of the artist, reminisces about the adventure of Marcelle's posing nude on the open shore: "In two paintings depicting Marcelle, she was unencumbered by the 'bathing dress' that appears in 'Girl in Blue' [*On the Beach*] — and I well remember my grandmother's telling me of her assigned task, which was to stand guard at the top of the dunes in order to warn Frieseke and his model if anyone was approaching."[2]

(continued on pg. 98)

On the Beach, by foregrounding themes of both nature and artifice, encapsulates the duality of Frieseke's artistic philosophy. On the one hand, he believed that a composition should be natural, rendered on the spot without fussy arrangement of forms, in order to capture the fleeting nature of light:

I do not believe in patching up a picture inside, after beginning it out-of-doors, nor do I believe in continuing a study from memory in the studio [nor] in constructing a picture from manifold studies which have been made in plein air. . . . *The longer I paint the stronger I feel we should be spontaneous.*[3]

In *On the Beach*, Frieseke suggests the importance of "naturalness" in painting through the subject of nature itself: sun-dappled, striated turquoise waves and golden sand, dimpled with footsteps, frame Marcelle, whose slender form casts a long midday shadow. As in many of his paintings, the horizon line disappears, compressing the female model within nature. Frieseke further indicates that Marcelle is "one" with nature by having her body bridge the sea and shore and by dressing her in the colors of the surrounding landscape: her ivory shoes blend into the sand, her blue dress and green cap echo the hues of the waves, and her floral tan parasol recalls the dotted tan beach. Marcelle turns into the sun toward the dunes as if responding to someone calling her name; Frieseke captures this casual and subtle movement, a snapshot in time.

Despite his insistence on the spontaneity of painting, Frieseke constructs his compositions deliberately, which, as some critics noted, often produced a synthetic or decorative quality:

His light hardly seems to be plein air *light at all. In fact it seems entirely artificial . . . a stunning concoction of blues and magentas frosted with early summer green and flecks of white.*[4]

Whatever [Mr. Frieseke] does has a sense of design, color, and style. A sense of gayety, an entertaining and well considered pattern, a remarkable knowledge of the effect of outdoor light on color are found in nearly all of his most recent paintings.[5]

Indeed, a closer study of *On the Beach* reveals Frieseke's conscious ordering of colors and shapes: with an edited palette of blues and creams, he superimposes ivory parasol on turquoise waves and blue dress and shadows on ivory beach. Anchoring the composition, Marcelle's vertical form intersects the diagonal lines of water and ground, and together with her shadow and the stretched-out cloth behind her, she creates linear "spokes," much like the ribs in her parasol. Too, the circles of the parasol and of the flecked sand in the foreground counterbalance the lines of Marcelle's body and of the waves. This compositional artifice is symbolized by Marcelle's own artifice, as she is playing dress-up with props of parasol, drapery, and stool. In fact a working-class model, Marcelle wears the beach attire of a wealthy tourist, and her Japanese umbrella further connotes upper middle-class luxury, as well as exoticism and decorativeness. Far from a quick snapshot, *On the Beach* is a precisely crafted scene where Marcelle, herself a decorative object, boldly holds the viewer's gaze, showing off her beauty within an equally beautiful setting.

1: Interview with Clara T. MacChesney, published on June 7, 1914.
2: Letter from Nicholas Kilmer to the current owner, October 15, 1989.
3: N. Kilmer, *Frederick Carl Frieseke: The Evolution of an American Impressionist*, Savannah, Georgia, 2001, p. 93.
4: W. Gerdts, "Frederick Carl Frieseke 1874," Butler Institute of American Art.
5: *The New York Times*, June 27, 1915, in Kilmer, p. 95.

64055

THEODORE WENDEL
(American, 1859-1932)
Ipswich, Marshes, circa 1900
Oil on canvas
38-1/2 x 31-1/2 inches (97.8 x 80.0 cm)
Signed lower right: *Theo Wendel*

PROVENANCE:
Private collection, Florida, *circa* 1905.

EXHIBITED:
Sofia, Bulgaria, "Exhibition of American Paintings in the Residence of United States Ambassador to Bulgaria," 2003;
Sullivan Goss Gallery, Santa Barbara, California, "The Summer Impressionists Show," 2013 (label verso).

LITERATURE:
W.H. Gerdts, *American Impressionism*, New York, 1984, pp. 63, 65;
Exhibition of American Paintings in the Residence of United States Ambassador to Bulgaria, exhibition catalogue, Sofia, Bulgaria, 2003, p. 12, illustrated.

Theodore Wendel is reputed as the premier Impressionist landscape painter of the Boston School, and is often considered the "most French" of American painters alongside Theodore Robinson and Childe Hassam.

Wendel grew up in Midway, Ohio, enrolling at the University of Cincinnati's School of Design in 1876. While there, he met Joseph DeCamp, and the two artists traveled to Germany in 1878 to study at the Munich Academy, where Wendel's academic style won him a medal. The artist then went on to Pölling, Bavaria to join Frank Duveneck's artist colony, traveling with the group to Florence and Venice where he was exposed to the Tonalist work of James McNeill Whistler. In 1887 Wendel visited Giverny, France, where he became heavily influenced by the Impressionist painter Claude Monet. While in Giverny Wendel adopted the French master's bright color and sketchy technique that he applied to the landscapes he subsequently painted when he settled in Boston. Dr. William H. Gerdts writes: "He [a critic in 1891] concluded that 'Mr. Wendel comes the nearest of the Bostonian Impressionists to handling the Monet style with effect. Wendel continued to exploit Impressionist color in his paintings of Gloucester and Ipswich, and he came to be regarded more as a devoted interpreter of the New England scene than as a stylistic innovator, though he remained faithful to the new aesthetic he had pioneered.' He [Wendel] was named the foremost Boston artist working in the style of Monet."[1]

1: *American Impressionism,* New York, 1984, pp. 63, 65.

Estimate: $20,000-$30,000

64056
JULIAN ALDEN WEIR (American, 1852-1919)
The Beach, Nassau, circa 1914
Oil on canvas
25-1/4 x 30-1/4 inches (64.1 x 76.8 cm)

PROVENANCE:
The artist;
Wife of the above;
Richard K. Larcada Gallery, New York;
Meredith Long & Co., Houston, Texas (labels verso);
Private collection, Baltimore, Maryland, *circa* 1965.

LITERATURE:
D. Phillips, *Julian Alden Weir: An Appreciation of His Life and Works*, New York, 1921, p. 136.

J. Alden Weir studied in Paris with the great academician Jean-Léon Gérôme, and at that time expressed his revulsion toward the then *avant-garde* of the French Impressionists. It was a position he later recanted. Weir became identified with the Impressionist movement in the United States, and was known for his landscapes and still-life paintings. In 1888, John Twachtman joined his friend in Branchville, Connecticut. At this time, Weir began a series of landscapes that were done of the sea around his farm, and were influenced by Twachtman's style of painting, moody and delicate, in a muted palette and limited range of values. Over the next few years, Weir's work evolved, influenced by his deepening interest in Impressionism, and perhaps, energized by his own success. The work became more atmospheric and was done in pale hues with broader brushwork. After about 1890, Weir seems to have lost interest in the theme of still-lives, although some continued to appear sporadically during the 1890s and 1900s. Around 1914, Weir traveled to Nassau in the Bahamas, where he produced many wonderful works depicting this exotic island. Dorothy Weir Young, the artist's daughter, in her book, *The Life and Letters of J. Alden Weir* (New Haven, Connecticut, 1960, p. 240) writes: "Canvases brought back from trips to Nassau were alive with Caribbean sunshine." *The Beach, Nassau* is one of his most beautiful paintings done in Nassau and the quote from the artist's letter to his daughter precisely sums up Weir's delight in his Caribbean travels.

Estimate: $20,000-$30,000

64057

WILLIAM SERGEANT KENDALL (American, 1869-1938)
Portrait of Mildred Stokes, 1901
Oil on canvas laid down on board
40 x 32 inches (101.6 x 81.3 cm)

PROVENANCE:
The artist;
Mildred Stokes, acquired from the above;
By descent through the family of the above.

EXHIBITED:
United States Embassy, Moscow, Russia,"The Art in Embassies Program," July 2010-June 2011.

LITERATURE:
United States Embassy, *The Art in Embassies Program*, exhibition catalogue, Moscow Russia, 2010, pp. 12-13, illustrated.

Mildred E. Phelps Stokes was a member of the highly prominent Anson Phelps Stokes family of New York. She had four brothers and four sisters. Her oldest brother, Isaac Newton Phelps Stokes and his wife were painted by John Singer Sargent in 1897 (The Metropolitan Museum of Art, New York). As a member of one of the wealthiest families in America at the turn of the century, Mildred wears an exquisitely detailed and undoubtedly fashionable dress with matching fan. Kendall had sent Mildred a letter from his studio at 26 West Eight Street dated April 14, 1901: "Dear Miss Stokes: Shall you be able to pose for me tomorrow-Monday-morning? I shall be ready for you any time after half-past ten, in the chance of you coming bring with you any old fan you may happen to have; as I may want to use it. Sincerely yours, William Sargeant Kendall."

Estimate: $6,000-$8,000

64058

HUBERT VOS (American, 1855-1935)
Ceramic Vase on Table, 1954
Oil on canvas
30 x 24 inches (76.2 x 61.0 cm)
Signed and dated lower right: *Hubert Vos / 1954*

Estimate: $3,000-$4,000

64059

HUGH HENRY BRECKENRIDGE (American, 1870-1937)
Portrait of a Lady
Oil on canvas
64 x 48 inches (162.6 x 121.9 cm)
Sighed lower left: *Hugh Breckenridge*

Estimate: $15,000-$25,000

64060

LOUIS BETTS (American, 1873-1961)
Portrait of Gertrude, 1926
Oil on canvas
30 x 25 inches (76.2 x 63.5 cm)
Signed upper left: *Louis Betts*
Inscribed and dated verso: *Gertrude Allen / Age 4 1/2 years / 1926*

PROVENANCE:
The artist;
Private collection, Chicago, Illinois, commissioned from the above *circa* 1930;
By descent to present owner.

Estimate: $3,000-$5,000

64061

MARTHA WALTER (American, 1875-1976)
Portrait of a Young Boy and His Toy Train, circa 1910
Oil on canvas
67-1/2 x 21-1/2 inches (171.5 x 54.6 cm)

PROVENANCE:
Private collection, *circa* 1950s.

The present work is one of Walter's signature images of children, among the subjects for which she is best known. In this arresting portrait, the artist captures the delight of a young blond child who has just been presented with a toy train. Distinct from Walter's more casual depictions of mothers and children on the beach or at Ellis Island, the present work is clearly a formal portrait, likely to have been commissioned for the home of an affluent client, given the child's elegant costume and the portrait's grand size. In style and format, it recalls the work of Walter's teacher William Merritt Chase (1849-1916).

Estimate: $15,000-$20,000

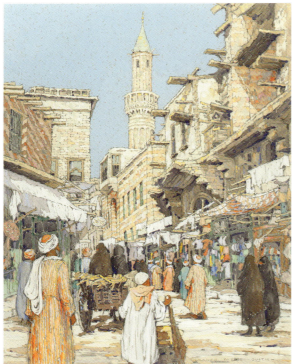

64062
ELEANOR PARKE CUSTIS (American, 1897-1983)
Street Scene, Cairo, Egypt
Gouache and pencil on paper
25-1/2 x 19-7/8 inches (64.8 x 50.5 cm)
Signed in pencil lower right: *Eleanor Parke Custis*

PROVENANCE:
Estate of the artist;
Anderson Galleries, Beverly Hills, California (label verso).

Estimate: $2,500-$3,500

64063
MARCUS WATERMAN (American, 1834-1914)
Mosque de Sidi Abdel Rahman
Oil on canvas
16 x 12 inches (40.6 x 30.5 cm)
Signed lower left: *Waterman*
Artist's label with title verso

NOTE:
This painting is housed in a Carrig-Rohane frame, signed, dated 1918 and numbered #1831B.

Estimate: $2,000-$3,000

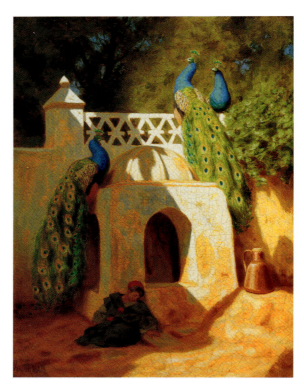

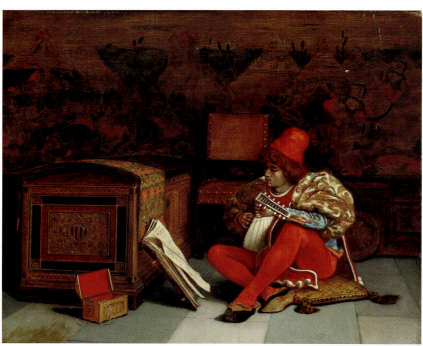

64064
CHARLES CARYL COLEMAN (American, 1840-1928)
Boy with Lute
Oil on canvas
9-1/4 x 11-1/2 inches (23.5 x 29.2 cm)

PROVENANCE:
Joseph Sartor Galleries, Dallas (label verso).

Estimate: $4,000-$6,000

64065

MURRAY PERCIVAL BEWLEY (American, 1884-1964)
Gloria
Oil on canvasboard
13-7/8 x 12 inches (35.2 x 30.5 cm)
Signed lower right: *Murray Bewley*

EXHIBITED:
William Macbeth, Inc., New York, "Paintings by American Artists," n.d. no. 434 (label verso).

Estimate: $4,000-$6,000

64066

ANNA BROWN (American, active 1890-1920)
The Reader
Oil on canvas
18-3/8 x 22-3/8 inches (46.7 x 56.8 cm)
Signed lower right: *A.W. Brown*

PROVENANCE:
Estate of the artist.

EXHIBITED:
Santa Fe East Gallery, Santa Fe East, New Mexico, "Five American Women Impressionists," 1982.

LITERATURE:
A.S. King, *Five American Women Impressionists*, exhibition catalogue, Santa Fe East Gallery, Santa Fe, New Mexico, 1982, pp. 19, 37, illustrated.

Estimate: $2,500-$3,500

64067

CAROLINE A. LORD (American, 1860-1928)
Seated Woman (Reflection), 1913
Oil on canvas
36-1/4 x 23 inches (92.1 x 58.4 cm)
Signed and dated lower right: *C.A. Lord / 1913*

PROVENANCE:
David Dike Gallery, Dallas (label verso).

EXHIBITED:
The Massillon Museum, Massillion, Ohio, and elsewhere, "Breaking with Tradition: Ohio Women Painters, 1870-1950", May 21-August 7, 2005, pp. 22, fig. 26, illustrated.

Estimate: $1,500-$2,000

64068

**HENRY HERMAN CROSS
(American, 1837-1918)**
Chestnut Racehorse with Jockey Up on a Training Track with a Wooded Landscape Beyond, 1892
Oil on canvas
28 x 36 inches (71.1 x 91.4 cm)
Signed and dated lower left: *H.H. Cross / 1892*

PROVENANCE:
The artist;
Marcus Daly, Riverside, Montana, commissioned from the above, 1891;
Estate of the above, 1900;
Baroness Margit Sigray Bessenyey, Montana, granddaughter of Marcus Daly, 1941;
Francis Bessenyey, stepson of the above, 1984;
Private collection, 1987.

Estimate: $4,000-$6,000

PROPERTY FROM THE COLLECTION OF MR. & MRS. EDWARD M. JONES III

64069
CHARLES CARY RUMSEY (American, 1879-1922)
Good and Plenty, 1907
Bronze with brown patina
13-1/4 inches (33.7 cm) high
Inscribed on the base: *CC Rumsey*
Inscribed on the base: *"Good and Plenty" / 5 CF*

LITERATURE:
The Burchfield Center for Western New York Art, *Charles Cary Rumsey, 1879-1922*, Buffalo, New York, 1983, p. 30, fig. 37 (another example illustrated).

The present work was cast in an edition of twenty-five.

Estimate: $10,000-$15,000

64070
CHARLES CARY RUMSEY (American, 1879-1922)
Polo Player on Pony: Skiddy von Stade
Bronze with brown patina
18-3/4 inches (47.6 cm) high
Inscribed on the base: *CC Rumsey / 12 CF*

LITERATURE:
The Burchfield Center for Western New York Art,
Charles Cary Rumsey, 1879-1922, Buffalo, New York, 1983, p. 33, fig. 64 (another example illustrated).

Skiddy von Stade was one of Long Island's most famous polo players, as well as a member of the Meadowbrook Polo Club with Rumsey.

Estimate: $10,000-$15,000

64071
CHARLES CARY RUMSEY (American, 1879-1922)
Polo Player on Pony: Harrison Tweed, circa 1910-12
Bronze with brown patina
19 inches (48.3 cm) high
Inscribed on the base: *CC Rumsey / 12 CF*

LITERATURE:
The Burchfield Center for Western New York Art,
Charles Cary Rumsey, 1879-1922, Buffalo, New York, 1983, p. 33, fig. 63 (another example illustrated).

Harrison Tweed was a polo player and member of the Meadowbrook Polo Club, as well as a friend of Charles Rumsey.

Estimate: $10,000-$15,000

64072

CHARLES CARY RUMSEY (American, 1879-1922)
Calf and Colt, 1907
Bronze with brown patina
7-1/4 inches (18.4 cm) high
Inscribed along the base: *CC Rumsey / 2/25*

LITERATURE:
The Burchfield Center for Western New York Art, *Charles Cary Rumsey, 1879-1922*, Buffalo, New York, 1983, p. 30, fig. 20 (another example illustrated).

Estimate: $4,000-$6,000

64073

CHARLES CARY RUMSEY (American, 1879-1922)
Dog Scratching, 1912
Bronze with brown patina
6-1/2 inches (16.5 cm) high
Inscribed on the base: *CC Rumsey / 1 CF*

LITERATURE:
The Burchfield Center for Western New York Art, *Charles Cary Rumsey, 1879-1922*, Buffalo, New York, 1983, p. 36, fig. 28 (another example illustrated).

Estimate: $2,500-$3,500

64074

CHARLES CARY RUMSEY (American, 1879-1922)
Horse and Man Drinking
Bronze with brown patina
6 inches (15.2 cm) high
Inscribed along the base: *CC Rumsey*
Stamped on the base: C. Valsuani Cire Perdue foundry
Inscribed along the base: *ROMAN BRONZE WORKS N.Y.*

The present work was cast in an edition of twenty-five.

Estimate: $4,000-$6,000

64075

CHARLES CARY RUMSEY (American, 1879-1922)
Horse Scratching
Bronze with brown patina
8-1/2 inches (21.6 cm) high

LITERATURE:
The Burchfield Center for Western New York Art, *Charles Cary Rumsey, 1879-1922*, Buffalo, New York, 1983, p. 33, fig. 42 (another example illustrated).

Estimate: $1,500-$2,000

64076

CHARLES CARY RUMSEY (American, 1879-1922)
Small Buffalo
Bronze with brown patina
5-3/4 inches (14.6 cm)
Inscribed on the base: *CC Rumsey*

Estimate: $2,000-$3,000

64077

CHARLES CARY RUMSEY (American, 1879-1922)
End of the Trail, 1904
Bronze with brown patina
26-1/2 inches (67.3 cm) high
Inscribed on the base: *CC Rumsey CF 2*

LITERATURE:
The Burchfield Center for Western New York Art, *Charles Cary Rumsey, 1879-1922*, Buffalo, New York, 1983, p. 29, fig. 30 (another example illustrated).

Estimate: $15,000-$18,000

64078

CHARLES CARY RUMSEY (American, 1879-1922)
Horses Fighting, 1921
Bronze with brown patina
10 inches (25.4 cm) high
Inscribed on the base: *CC Rumsey / 1 CF*

LITERATURE:
The Burchfield Center for Western New York Art, *Charles Cary Rumsey, 1879-1922*, Buffalo, New York, 1983, p. 39, fig. 43 (another example illustrated).

Estimate: $5,000-$7,000

64079

**CHARLES CARY RUMSEY
(American, 1879-1922)**
Old Virginian, 1917
Bronze with brown patina
16 inches (40.6 cm) high
Inscribed on the base:
CC Rumsey / 3 CF

LITERATURE:
The Burchfield Center for Western New York Art, *Charles Cary Rumsey, 1879-1922*, Buffalo, New York, 1983, p. 42, fig. 51 (another example illustrated).

Estimate: $10,000-$15,000

64080

CHARLES CARY RUMSEY (American, 1879-1922)
Bull Bison
Bronze with brown patina
11-3/4 inches (29.8 cm) high
Inscribed on the base: *CC Rumsey*
Inscribed along the base: *Ed. 5/25*

Estimate: $4,000-$6,000

64081
**CHARLES CARY RUMSEY
(American, 1879-1922)**
Winning the Race
Bronze with brown patina
9-1/4 inches (23.5 cm) high
Inscribed along the base: *2 CF*

LITERATURE:
The Burchfield Center for Western New York Art, *Charles Cary Rumsey, 1879-1922*, Buffalo, New York, 1983, p. 32, fig. 82 (another example illustrated).

Estimate: $3,000-$5,000

64082
**CHARLES CARY RUMSEY
(American, 1879-1922)**
Colt Scratching Nose, 1916
Bronze with brown patina
6-1/2 inches (16.5 cm) high
Inscribed on the base: *CC Rumsey*

LITERATURE:
The Burchfield Center for Western New York Art, *Charles Cary Rumsey, 1879-1922*, Buffalo, New York, 1983, p. 37, fig. 24 (another example illustrated).

Estimate: $2,500-$3,500

64083

CHARLES CARY RUMSEY (American, 1879-1922)
Bouger Red, 1912
Bronze with brown patina
17 inches (43.2 cm) high
Inscribed along the base: *CC Rumsey*
Inscribed along base: *"Bouger Red" / MHR*

LITERATURE:
The Burchfield Center for Western New York Art, *Charles Cary Rumsey, 1879-1922*, Buffalo, New York, 1983, p. 36, fig. 10 (another example illustrated).

The present work is the artist's proof casting.

Estimate: $8,000-$12,000

64084

CHARLES CARY RUMSEY (American, 1879-1922)
Study for a Centaur, circa 1914
Bronze with brown patina
18-1/2 inches (47.0 cm) high

LITERATURE:
The Burchfield Center for Western New York Art, *Charles Cary Rumsey, 1879-1922*, Buffalo, New York, 1983, p. 35, fig. 23 (another example illustrated).

The present work was cast in an edition of twenty-five.

Estimate: $5,000-$7,000

64085

CHARLES CARY RUMSEY (American, 1879-1922)
Dancing Female Nude, 1910
Bronze with brown patina
9-3/4 inches (24.8 cm) high
Inscribed on the base: *CC Rumsey / 21 CF*

LITERATURE:
The Burchfield Center for Western New York Art, *Charles Cary Rumsey, 1879-1922*, Buffalo, New York, 1983, p. 32, fig. 26 (another example illustrated).

Estimate: $4,000-$6,000

64086

CHARLES CARY RUMSEY (American, 1879-1922)
Pan Piping
Bronze with brown patina
20-1/2 inches (52.1 cm) high
Inscribed on the base: *CC Rumsey*
Inscribed along the base: *CF 1*

LITERATURE:
The Burchfield Center for Western New York Art, *Charles Cary Rumsey, 1879-1922*, Buffalo, New York, 1983, p. 34, fig. 57 (another example illustrated).

Estimate: $10,000-$15,000

64087

MORGAN RUSSELL
(American, 1886-1953)
Innocence et Elegance
Oil on canvas
44 x 57 inches (111.8 x 144.8 cm)
Signed lower right: *Morgan Russell*
Signed and titled verso: *Morgan Russell / Innocence et Elegance*

PROVENANCE:
The artist;
By descent to the great, great grand niece of the above, Texas;
Private collection, California (acquired from the above circa 1980s);
By descent to the present owner, *circa* 1990s.

LITERATURE:
M.S. Kushner, *Morgan Russell: A Retrospective by Marilyn S. Kushner*, New York, 1990, p. 160, pl. 160, illustrated;
Decoration Internationale, June 1983, Edition 62, pp. 95, 100.

Estimate: $4,000-$6,000

64088

WILLIAM MEYEROWITZ
(American, 1887-1981)
Gloucester, circa 1920
Oil on canvas laid down on board
18 x 22 inches (45.7 x 55.9 cm)
Signed lower right: *Wm. Meyerowitz*

PROPERTY OF A DISTINGUISHED PRIVATE COLLECTOR

PROVENANCE:
The artist;
Moshe Dlunowsky, acquired from the above;
By descent;
Sotheby's, New York, *American Paintings, Drawings and Sculpture*, September 24, 2008, lot 112;
Acquired by the present owner from the above.

Estimate: $4,000-$6,000

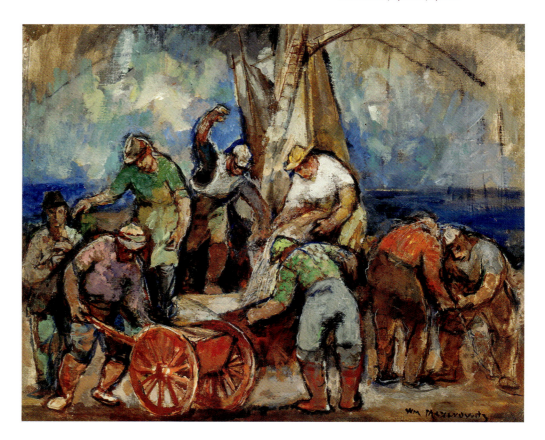

64089

MAX WEBER
(American, 1881-1961)
Bathers, 1910
Gouache on paper laid down on cardstock
9-3/4 x 7 inches
(24.8 x 17.8 cm) (sheet)
Signed and dated in pencil in lower right margin:
Max Weber 1910

PROPERTY FROM A DISTINGUISHED PRIVATE COLLECTOR

PROVENANCE:
Private collection, New York;
ACA Galleries, New York;
Forum Gallery, New York (labels verso);
Acquired by the present owner from the above, 2009.

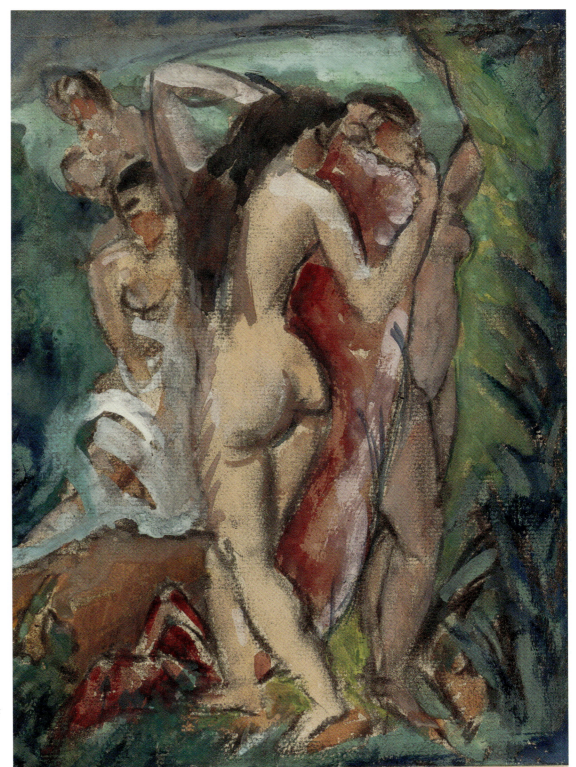

Bathers is a stellar example of Max Weber's work during the pivotal period from 1909 to 1912, when he transitioned from his early Fauvist compositions to his mature Cubist style. Painted in 1910, two years after Weber returned to New York from his studies in Europe, the work retains the foundation of his European training, but the contorted figures and flattened space embody the fundamental roots for his Cubist exploration, which he would continue to develop, and lead to the most prolific and successful decade of his career.

Estimate: $60,000-$80,000

64090

THOMAS HART BENTON (American, 1889-1975)
Slave Master with Slaves (Study for The American Historical Epic), circa 1924-27
Crayon with pencil and ink on paper
15-1/2 x 17-1/2 inches (39.4 x 44.5 cm) (sheet)
Signed lower right: *Benton*

PROVENANCE:
The artist;
Robert E. Neuse, New York, acquired from the above;
The Neuse family, New York, by descent;
Acquired by the present owner from the above.

We are grateful to Dr. Henry Adams, Professor of American Art at Case Western Reserve University in Cleveland, Ohio, for authenticating this drawing as an autograph work by Benton, and for generously providing important provenance information essential to the cataloguing of this lot.

This large, highly-finished sheet is a major rediscovery in Thomas Hart Benton's drawing oeuvre and relates directly to *Slavery*, one of the toughest thematic panels in his very first mural—*The American Historical Epic* (circa 1924-29). The overseer whipping slaves with a church spire directly behind him in the far right background is the kind of juxtaposition Benton was bold enough to install in so many of his murals, motifs that are loaded with virulent social criticism for which he was often savagely criticized. Benton came from a long line of distinguished politicians who grappled with tough social issues, and in his own way, within in realm of art, the artist carried on his family's legacy for substantive debate. Interestingly, the artist's namesake, U.S. Senator Thomas Hart Benton (1782-1858), fought hard against the extension of slavery into U.S. territories where it had not previously existed.

Notably, this drawing reduces the figures to cubic forms showing the play of light and dark on them, a testament to the likely purpose of this sheet as either a final study for the mural panel or perhaps for a unexecuted lithograph based on it. Benton strove to achieve visual consistency in his complex murals as well as his lithographs by making sure that the light-dark contrasts were optically convincing. The use of lithographic crayon with touches of ink is interesting here because it was around the early 1920s that Benton first began making lithographic prints of his compositions. This led to an arrangement with Associated American Artists Gallery in New York which sold limited editions of them (250) by subscription.

The first owner of this impressive sheet was New Yorker Robert E. Neuse. As Henry Adams has noted, "Robert E. Neuse was dealer in rare books who connected with Thomas Hart Benton sometime shortly before the First World War. Neuse became Benton's landlord in New York in the 1920s and early 1930s, and also rented an apartment to Jackson Pollock and his brothers. About 1922 Benton designed a bookplate for him, which sometimes surfaces in books sold on ebay, and he often seems to have paid his rent in works of art, which may have been the case with the present work. Neuse eventually moved to western Massachusetts and correspondence survives in which he attempted to lure Benton to settle nearby. By this time, however, Benton had purchased land on Martha's Vineyard, and settled there instead. Neuse's wife Josephine wrote a book on gardening, *The Country Garden*, which is still in print."

Estimate: $30,000-$50,000

64091

THOMAS HART BENTON (American, 1889-1975)
Cradling Wheat, 1939
Lithograph on paper
10-1/4 x 12-3/8 inches (26.0 x 31.4 cm) (sight)
Ed. 250
Signed in pencil in lower margin: *Benton*
Circulated by Associated American Artists, New York (label verso)

LITERATURE:
C. Fath, *The Lithographs of Thomas Hart Benton*, London and Austin, Texas, 1979, pp. 74, no. 27, (another example illustrated).

This lithograph is after a painting, also titled *Cradling Wheat*, created in 1938, which is in the City Art Museum of St. Louis, Missouri.

Estimate: $2,000-$3,000

64092

DALE NICHOLS (American, 1904-1995)
Winter Farm Scene
Pastel and gouache on paper
10-3/4 x 13-3/4 inches (27.3 x 34.9 cm) (sight)
Signed lower right: *Dale Nichols*

Estimate: $4,000-$6,000

64093

JULIA PEARL (American, 20th Century)
Two Boys, 1950
Oil on canvas
30 x 36 inches (76.2 x 91.4 cm)
Signed and dated in pencil on verso: *Julia Pearl / February 3, 1950*

PROVENANCE:
The Little Gallery, Newark, New Jersey (stamp on stretcher);
Private collection, Dallas.

We wish to thank the California artist Ivan Majdrakoff, Julia Pearl's former husband, for his gracious assistance in cataloguing this painting.

Julia Pearl painted this sensitive portrait of boys riding piggyback in 1950, when she was a graduate student in her twenties at the Cranbrook Academy of Art in Bloomfield Hills, Michigan. Her early work reflects the figurative and social realist influence of Robert Gwathmey and Ben Shahn, particularly in its use of minimalist forms to convey complex human emotions. After Cranbrook, Julia returned to New York City and married her high school classmate, the fellow artist Ivan Majdrakoff. The couple was close friends of the avant-garde Beat poet Gerd Stern, with whom they continued to collaborate after moving to the California Bay Area: for Stern's 1952 *First Poems and Others*, Ivan did the illustrations and Julia, the calligraphy. In California, during the 1960s, Pearl abandoned figurative painting in favor of an organic abstraction. Sometime before her death (likely in the 1990s), Pearl destroyed her paintings, explaining why her work rarely appears on the market. Several of her abstractions are in private collections, but as a surviving early figurative work, *Two Boys* is an extraordinary discovery.

Estimate: $3,000-$5,000

64094
CHARLES EPHRAIM BURCHFIELD (American, 1893-1967)
Autumn Flowers, circa 1955-60
Watercolor on paper
30 x 22 inches (76.2 x 55.9 cm)
Signed with initials in monogram and dated lower left: *CB 1955-60*

PROVENANCE:
Frank Rehn Gallery, New York (label verso);
Private collection, Gulfport, Mississippi.

Estimate: $100,000-$150,000

64095

MILTON AVERY (American, 1885-1965)
Three Figures, 1946
Pen and brown ink on paper
13-7/8 x 16-3/4 inches (35.2 x 42.5 cm) (sheet)
Signed and dated in pen lower right: *Milton Avery / 1946*
Inscribed and dated in pen verso: *Three Figures 14 x 17 1946*

PROVENANCE:
Swann Galleries, New York, *American Art*, June 8, 2006, lot 6.

Estimate: $5,000-$7,000

64096

MILTON AVERY (American, 1893-1965)
Setting Sun, 1959
Oil on paper
22-1/2 x 17 inches (57.2 x 43.2 cm)
Signed and dated lower left: *Milton Avery 1959*

PROVENANCE:
The artist;
Grace Borgenicht Gallery, New York;
Private collection, acquired from the above, 1986;
By descent to the present owner from the above.

Estimate: $20,000-$30,000

64097

CHARLES EPHRAIM BURCHFIELD (American, 1893-1967)
Noon in September, 1916
Watercolor and pencil on paper
8-7/8 x 11-7/8 inches
(22.5 x 30.2 cm) (sheet)
Signed and dated in pencil lower right: *C. Burchfield - 1916*
Inscribed verso: *noon in September / Sept 10, 1916*

PROVENANCE:
Private collection, New York;
By descent to the present owner.

Estimate: $6,000-$8,000

64098

CHARLES EPHRAIM BURCHFIELD (American, 1893-1967)
Rising Fog in Winter, 1917
Watercolor and pencil on paper
14 x 11 inches (35.6 x 27.9 cm) (sheet)
Signed and dated in pencil lower left: *Chas Burchfield / 1917*
Inscribed verso: *rising fog in winter*

PROVENANCE:
Private collection, New York;
By descent to the present owner.

Estimate: $4,000-$6,000

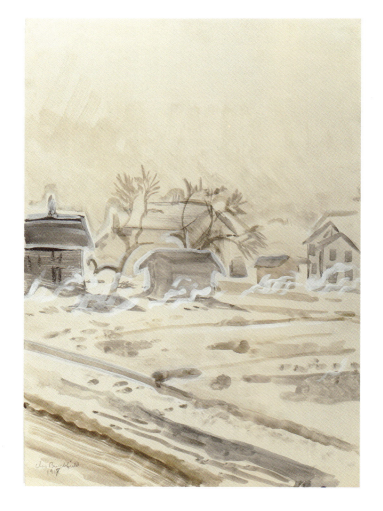

64099

CHARLES EPHRAIM BURCHFIELD (American, 1893-1967)
Tree in a Landscape
Watercolor and pencil on paper
26-7/8 x 19-1/8 inches (68.3 x 48.6 cm) (sheet)

PROVENANCE:
Private collection, New York;
By descent to the present owner.

Estimate: $12,000-$18,000

64100
ANNA HYATT HUNTINGTON (American, 1876-1973)
Torch Bearers, 1955; cast in 1962
Bronze with natural verdigris patina
186 inches (472.4 cm) high
Inscribed on the base: *a Hyatt Huntington/Stanerigg 1953 © / ROMAN BRONZE WORKS INC NY*

PROPERTY FROM THE DISCOVERY MUSEUM AND PLANETARIUM, WITH PROCEEDS TO DIRECTLY BENEFIT SCIENCE AND ENGINEERING EDUCATIONAL PROGRAMS AND EXHIBITS

PROVENANCE:
The artist;
The Museum of Art, Science and Industry, Bridgeport, Connecticut, gift from the above, 1962.

LITERATURE:
M.G. Eden, *Energy and Individuality in the Art of Anna Hyatt Huntington, Sculptor, and Amy Beach, Composer*, Metuchen, New Jersey, 1987, p. 230-31;
J. Conner and K. Rosenkranz, *Rediscoveries in American* Sculpture, Austin, Texas, 1989, p, 77;
M.A. Bzdak, *Public Sculpture in New Jersey: Monuments to Collective Identity*, New Brunswick, New Jersey, 1999, p. 143.

Estimate: $400,000-$600,000

Anna Hyatt Huntington, acclaimed as one of the most successful female sculptor in American history, is renowned for her portrayal of animals. Her work, on large and small scale, can be found in the collections of over 250 museums, parks and public gardens worldwide. Conceived in 1955 and executed in 1962, *Torch Bearer* is one of only five known casts, and is the most important of Huntington's works to ever come to auction.

The daughter of Alpheus Hyatt, an eminent paleontologist and Harvard University professor, Huntington had the opportunity growing up to familiarize herself with all varieties of savage and domestic animals. Her sympathy for animals and understanding of their anatomy was fostered, first, by study with Henry Kitson in Boston, and then as a pupil at the Art Students League of New York City where she received instruction from Hermon Atkins MacNeil and criticism from Gutzon Borglum, a noted animal sculptor of the day. She rounded out her artistic education by modeling domestic animals on a farm at Porto Bello, Maryland, and the wild animals at the New York Zoological Park. "Animals," she said, "have many moods and to represent them is a joy."[1] Huntington's ability to capture the essence of living creatures soon translated into small bronzes and commissions.

By 1907 Huntington was working steadily in France and Italy, and in 1910 she had already made the model for *Joan of Arc*, her earliest notable monument and the first heroic equestrian statue of a woman. The work, which depicts a slender, armor-clad Joan of Arc astride a spirited steed and holding her sword of destiny aloft, won an honorable mention at the Paris Salon of 1910. Historian Charlotte Streifer Rubinstein notes: "Recognized as one of the finest equestrian statues by an American, Joan of Arc compares favorably with versions by the Frenchmen Fremiet and DuBois...[and is] a landmark in the history of women sculptors."[2]

Huntington's series of famed equestrian statues continued with *Cid Campeador*, 1927, in Seville, Spain and of the Hispanic Society of America in New York City. Her *Don Quixote* of 1942 is also part of the permanent collection of Hispanic Society. In each of these works, Huntington demonstrates her rare ability to adapt the character of the horse to that of the individual horseman, while treating both subjects with real feeling for their inherent dignity. *Torch Bearers*-symbolizing the passing of the torch of civilization and progress from one generation to the next-embodies this same genius for modeling, for direct expression of action, as well as the artist's unparalleled gift of observation.

Huntington originally conceived of *Torch Bearers* in 1955 to be offered as a unique gift from the artist and her husband, Archer Milton Huntington, to the University of Madrid, in Spain. In October 1961 Earle M. Newton, Director of The Museum of Art, Science and Industry in Bridgeport, Connecticut, wrote to Huntington requesting a suitable monument to be placed in the institution's courtyard. Huntington responded within days that the project interested her, and she suggested *Torch Bearers*. The artist ultimately offered the work as a gift to the new museum, along with an additional $5,000 toward the cost of the base, in order to ensure a proper setting for her grand masterwork.

The museum board was thrilled with the gift, and they immediately appointed a landscape architect to select and prepare the perfect plot for the monument on the institution's grounds. In a letter to the artist dated March 1, 1962, Newton writes: "[We have] already selected the position and will be laying out the mounting as soon as the frost breaks this spring. I think it's a very lovely spot, with a backing of foliage; I am sure you will like it. And we are so pleased to have this superb piece of art."

Roman Bronze Works was hired to cast the work in bronze, an undertaking which took months to complete. Finally, On August 6, 1963, the museum unveiled a one-

woma
Bearer
Museu

The m
when
today.
Septer
at the
would
a huge
large
We ar
next s
provi

"As a
averag
to 1,7(
a little

In ad
of *Tor*
are lo
Steven
Chrys

Throu
public
placed
of 97,
remai
its gra
celebr
greate

Please
an ap
avival
de-ins

1: as o
Nature
2: *Am*
Dimer

"Let
to fi
pass
bor
disc
thei
or p
righ
com
tod

John

64101

WILLIAM ZORACH (American, 1887-1966)
French Cottage, circa 1910-12
Oil on board
7-1/4 x 7-3/8 inches (18.4 x 18.7 cm)
Bears inscription verso by the son of the artist: *Painted in France / 1910-12 / by William Zorach / per Tessim Zorach / 12/9/76*

Estimate: $2,000-$3,000

64102

GUSTAVE CIMIOTTI (American, 1875-1969)
The Brook, Near Caldwell, New Jersey, circa 1930
Oil on artists' board
7-1/2 x 10-1/2 inches (19.1 x 26.7 cm)
Signed lower left: *Cimiotti*
Inscribed with title verso

PROVENANCE:
The artist;
Mr. Arthur O. Townsend, Montclair, New Jersey, gift from the above, 1931.

NOTE:
A handwritten letter from the artist to Mr. Arthur O. Townsend, Montclair, New Jersey, dated December 22, 1931 is attached to the artwork verso.

Estimate: $2,000-$3,000

64103

CHARLES HERBERT WOODBURY (American, 1864-1940)
Sun on Narrow Cove, Ogunquit, circa 1910
Oil on canvasboard
10 x 13-7/8 inches (25.4 x 35.2 cm)
Signed lower right: *Charles H. Woodbury*
Bears signature verso

PROPERTY FROM A DISTINGUISHED PRIVATE COLLECTOR

PROVENANCE:
M. Ford Creech Antiques, Memphis, Tennessee;
Acquired by the present owner from the above, 2008.

Estimate: $3,000-$5,000

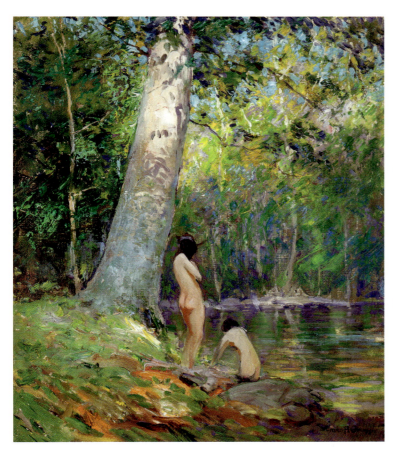

64104
EMILE ALBERT GRUPPE (American, 1896-1978)
Bathers in a Wooded Landscape
Oil on canvas
24 x 20-1/2 inches (61.0 x 52.1 cm)
Signed lower right: *Emile A. Gruppe*

PROVENANCE:
Private collection, Massachusetts.

Estimate: $3,000-$5,000

64105
JOSEPH TOMANEK (American, 1889-1974)
Conversation by the Lake
Oil on board
16 x 12 inches (40.6 x 30.5 cm)
Signed lower left: *Tomanek*
Signed again and inscribed with artist's street address verso

NOTE:
This painting is housed in a period Newcomb-Macklin frame.

Estimate: $4,000-$6,000

64106

JONAS LIE (Norwegian/American, 1880-1940)
Land's End
Oil on canvas
30-1/4 x 60-1/4 inches (76.8 x 153.0 cm)
Signed lower left: *Jonas Lie*

PROVENANCE:
Spanierman Gallery, New York (label verso).

EXHIBITED:
National Academy of Design, New York, n.d.;
Corcoran Gallery of Art, New York, "Twelfth Exhibition of Contemporary American Oil Paintings," 1930-1931 (labels verso).

Estimate: $70,000-$90,000

64107

HAYLEY R. LEVER (American, 1876-1958)
Moonlight Over Smith's Cove, East Gloucester, circa 1920
Oil on canvas
20 x 24 inches (50.8 x 61.0 cm)
Signed lower left: *Hayley Lever*

PROPERTY FROM A DISTINGUISHED PRIVATE COLLECTOR

PROVENANCE:
Campanile Galleries, Chicago, Illinois;
Private collection, New York;
Godel & Co., New York (label verso);
Acquired by the present owner from the above, 2009.

Estimate: $40,000-$60,000

64108

AARON HARRY GORSON (American, 1872-1933)
Steel Mill at Night (Jones & Laughlin by Night)
Oil on board
20 x 16 inches (50.8 x 40.6 cm)
Signed lower left: *AH Gorson*

PROPERTY FROM A DISTINGUISHED COLLECTION, PITTSBURGH, PENNSYLVANIA

PROVENANCE:
J.J. Gillespie Company Fine Art Galleries, Pittsburgh, Pennsylvania (label verso);
Judge Thomas P. Trimble, Old Allegheny, Pennsylvania, purchased from the above before 1919;
By descent to Margaret Trimble, Pittsburgh, Pennsylvania;
Gifted from the above to her niece Mary Trimble on the occasion of her marriage to Dr. Raymond F. Brittain, Pittsburgh, Pennsylvania;
By descent to Victoria Brittain Payne, Pittsburgh, Pennsylvania;
By descent to the present owner.

Lithuanian-born Aaron Gorson's atmospheric masterwork *Steel Mill at Night* exemplifies his paintings of the iron and steel mills of Pittsburgh for which he became well known in the 1910s. Using a principal palette of blue-grays, he depicts one of the prominent mills along the Monongahela River, likely the Jones & Laughlin Steel Company, his favorite industrial subject. Rising up from a crescent-shaped bend in the Monongahela, the various mill structures — the factory with smokestacks and a coal hoist on the edge of the riverbank — emit luminous, yellow-peach vapors into the night sky. Along the opposite shore, a puff of smoke from a barge carrying hot iron further illuminates the darkness, while pinpoint lights signal the residential areas of Pittsburgh. In the right foreground, a weighty dock with a gangplank anchors the composition, providing a foil to the shimmery water and cloud elements. Cleverly and perhaps ironically, Gorson uses the heaviest impasto for the weightless smoke and lights and the thinnest washes for the massive buildings. *Steel Mill at Night* is thus a poetic study of gradations of light, tones, and volumes.

Indeed, rather than detailing the arduous and dirty manufacturing process in his paintings, Gorson focused, instead, on the aesthetics of the industrial landscape. In the early twentieth century, when he was working in Pittsburgh, the city was becoming an international force in the coal, iron, and steel industries. Huge plants like Jones & Laughlin, Duquesne Steel Works, and Homestead Steel Works stretched out along the banks of the Monongahela, Allegheny, and Ohio Rivers, which fed into Pittsburgh. Barges and trains further crowded the region, transporting coal and other supplies to the mills and foundries. "In 1909, the city produced as much pig iron as France, Russia, and Canada combined — 11% of the world's output."[1] Such rapid industrialization was not without strife for laborers — "the twelve-hour day and the seven-day week prevailed in the steel mills"[2] — and irritation for the general populace — "people scurried to their jobs through sooty streets, handkerchiefs clamped over noses and mouths to filter the dirty air."[3]

Yet Gorson, influenced by his training with James McNeill Whistler in Paris, saw nothing but beauty in this "city of smoke and cinders." From Whistler, Gorson adopted a tonal palette; loose brushwork; and an interest in fleeting atmospheric conditions, such as rain and fog at twilight or dusk. Like Whistler, he also titled his paintings after musical forms, for example, *Pittsburgh Nocturne*. Gorson's multiple paintings of a certain factory at different times of day and under different weather conditions also recalled the avant-garde techniques of Claude Monet and Paul Cézanne. While others of Gorson's contemporaries, including Otto Kuhler, John White Alexander, and Lewis Hine, chronicled the power of the factories and their toll on workers, Gorson showed Pittsburgh as "bountifully endowed by nature with scenes of grandeur and enthralling picturesqueness."[4]

Given Gorson's romanticized view of Pittsburgh's industry, it is not surprising that his most enthusiastic patrons were the city's leaders and manufacturing work, *Steel Mill at Night*, around 1919. Likewise, the steel magnate James B. Laughlin owned a *Nocturne*, and the president of United States Steel, Judge Elbert Henry Gary, raved about his Gorson painting, capturing a broad sentiment:

I continue to like the painting which I purchased from you a few years ago, "The Mills at Night, Pittsburgh, Pennsylvania." It shows in marked contrast the glare of light thrown out by furnaces on the distant shore of the river, and somber barges in the half darkness of the foreground. I consider it excellent, vivid and lifelike. I think it is a work of art that will endure.[5]

1: R. Younger, *The Power and the Glory: Pittsburgh Industrial Landscapes by Aaron Harry Gorson*, New York, 1989, p. 2.
2: Ibid, p. 2.
3: R. Wilson, "Painters of Pittsburgh . . . Aaron Harry Gorson," *Pittsburgh Press Roto*, July 31, 1977, p. 18.
4: C. Gillespie, "Pittsburgh the Beautiful: Artist Finds Inspiration for Pictures Amid the City's Smoke and Gasses," *Pittsburgh Press Illustrated Sunday Magazine Section*, June 7, 1908, p. 13.
5: E.H. Gary to A.H. Gorson, May 13, 1936, Gorson Documentation File.

Estimate: $20,000-$30,000

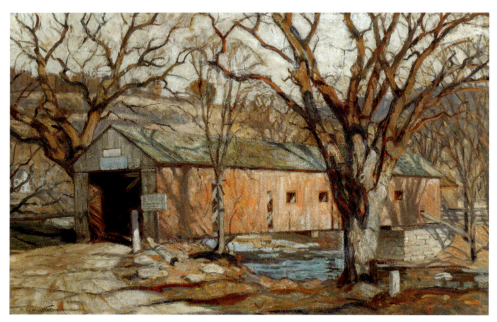

64109

ROBERT EMMETT OWEN
(American, 1878-1957)
The Covered Bridge
Oil on canvas
39-3/4 x 60-1/2 inches
(101.0 x 153.7 cm)
Signed lower left: *R Emmett Owen*

PROVENANCE:
Vose Galleries, Boston, Massachusetts (label verso).

Estimate: $4,000-$6,000

64110

GUY CARLETON WIGGINS
(American, 1883-1962)
Winter Brilliance, 1927
Oil on canvasboard
12 x 16 inches (30.5 x 40.6 cm)
Signed lower right: *Guy Wiggins*
Titled, signed, and dated verso: *"Winter Brilliance" / Guy Wiggins / 1927*
Inscribed on frame: *Guy Wiggins / 226 W. 59th St.*

PROVENANCE:
Private collection, New York.

We wish to thank Mr. Guy A. Wiggins for his gracious assistance in cataloguing this painting. In his letter of authenticity, which accompanies the lot, Mr. Wiggins writes, "My father probably painted this scene near our home in Lyme, Connecticut, where we lived part of the time during the nineteen twenties."

Estimate: $5,000-$7,000

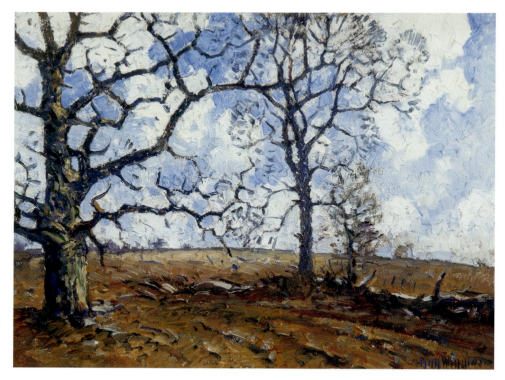

64111

ANTHONY THIEME
(American, 1888-1954)
Walking Home from Church, Rockport
Watercolor on paper
14-1/2 x 21-1/2 inches
(36.8 x 54.6 cm) (sight)
Signed lower right: *A. Thieme*

Estimate: $3,000-$5,000

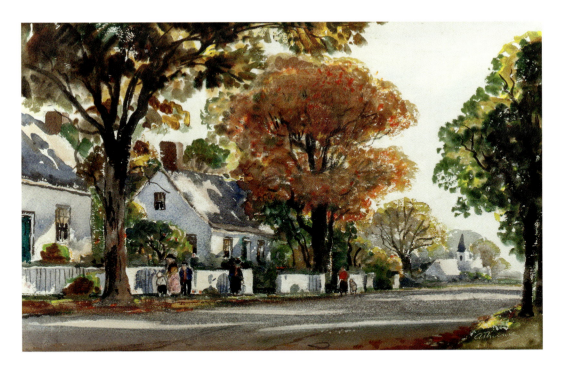

64112

ANTHONY THIEME
(American, 1888-1954)
Morning Light
Oil on canvas
25-1/4 x 30-1/4 inches
(64.1 x 76.8 cm)
Signed lower right: *AThieme*

Estimate: $10,000-$15,000

64113

HARRIET WHITNEY FRISHMUTH
(American, 1880-1980)
The Vine, modeled and cast 1921
Bronze with greenish-brown patina
12-1/4 inches (31.1 cm) high on 3/4 inches high marble base
Inscribed along the base: © / 1921 / HARRIET W. FRISHMUTH
Stamped with foundry mark along the base: GORHAM CO FOUNDERS / QBWS

PROPERTY FROM A DISTINGUISHED PRIVATE COLLECTOR

PROVENANCE:
Collection of Eleanor Ziegler, Lewes, Delaware;
Newman Galleries, Philadelphia, Pennsylvania (label under marble base);
Acquired by the present owner from the above, 2008.

LITERATURE:
C.S. Rubinstein, *American Women Sculptors*, Boston, Massachusetts, 1990, p. 155, another example illustrated;
J. Conner, L.R. Lehmbeck, T. Tolles, F.L. Hohmann III, *Captured Motion, The Sculpture of Harriet Whitney Frishmuth: A Catalogue of Works*, New York, 2006, pp. 29-33, 37, 46, 54, 58-59, 71, 79, 102, 150-51, 240, no. 1921:1 (another example illustrated).

One of Frishmuth's most commercially successful models, *The Vine* was awarded the Shaw Memorial Prize at the National Academy of Design in 1923. Desha, the artist's most frequently used model, and Renee Wilde, another dancer and model for Frishmuth, posed for the work.

Estimate: $10,000-$15,000

64114

HARRIET WHITNEY FRISHMUTH
(American, 1880-1980)
Desha, modeled 1927; cast 1927-65
Bronze with greenish-brown patina
14-1/2 inches (36.8 cm) high on 1/2 inches high marble base
Inscribed along the base: *HARRIET W FRISHMUTH 1927* ©
Stamped with foundry mark along the base: *GORHAM CO FOUNDERS / QFSK*

PROPERTY FROM A DISTINGUISHED PRIVATE COLLECTOR

PROVENANCE:
Private collection, Charlotte, North Carolina;
Freeman's, Philadelphia, Pennsylvania, December 7, 2008, lot 102;
Acquired by the present owner from the above.

LITERATURE:
C.N. Aronson, *Sculptured Hyacinths*, New York, 1973, pp. 47-49, 174, 179, 213, (another example illustrated);
The Gorham Company, Bronze Division, *Famous Small Bronzes*, New York, 1928, pp. 106-07, (another example illustrated);
P.G. Proske, *Brookgreen Gardens Sculpture*, Murrell's Inlet, South Carolina, 1968 edition, p. 224;
J. Conner, L.R. Lehmbeck, T. Tolles, F.L. Hohmann III, *Captured Motion, The Sculpture of Harriet Whitney Frishmuth: A Catalogue of Works*, New York, 2006, p. 254, no. 1927:5 (another example illustrated).

Desha Delteil (née Podgorska, 1900-1980) was the artist's most frequently used model. Arriving in America from Yugoslavia in 1914, Delteil danced with Michel Fokine's dance company. Delteil and Frishmuth were introduced in 1916 through Frances Grimes, a fellow sculptor who also used the dancer as a model. The lively pose exhibited here is typical of Desha's exuberance and talent as a dancer.

Estimate: $10,000-$15,000

64115

WALTER KOENIGER (American, 1881-1943)
Winter Landscape with Brook
Oil on canvas
24-1/8 x 30-1/8 inches
(61.3 x 76.5 cm)
Signed lower right: *W. Koeniger*

Estimate: $4,000-$6,000

64116

GRANDMA MOSES (American, 1860-1961)
The Wood Road, 1947
Tempera on panel
9 x 6 inches (22.9 x 15.2 cm)
Signed lower right: *Moses.*
Artist's label verso

PROVENANCE:
James Vigeveno Galleries, Los Angeles, California;
Butterfields, San Francisco, California, *American Paintings,* November 7, 1990, lot 3854 (labels verso).

Estimate: $5,000-$8,000

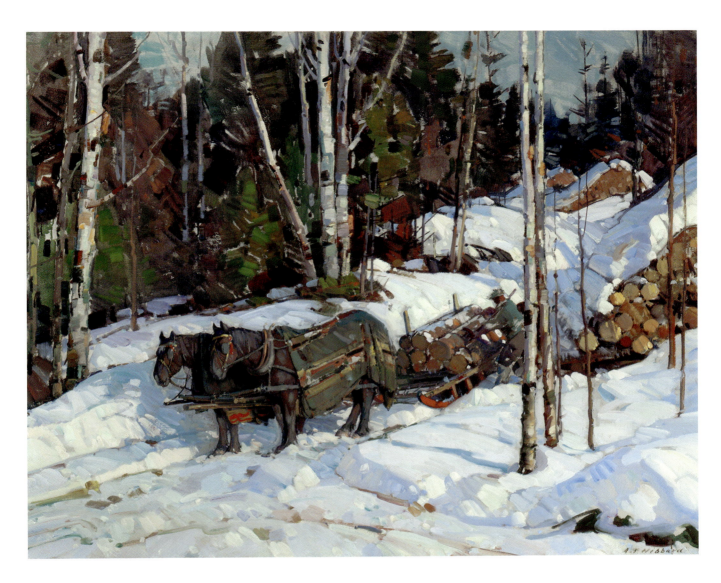

64117

ALDRO THOMPSON HIBBARD (American, 1886-1972)
Logging in Vermont
Oil on canvas laid on cradled panel
32-1/2 x 40-3/8 inches (82.6 x 102.6 cm)
Signed lower right: *A.T. Hibbard*

PROVENANCE:
Vose Galleries, Boston, Massachusetts (label verso);
Private collector, Massachusetts.

Estimate: $25,000-$35,000

64118

ARTHUR CLIFTON GOODWIN
(American, 1864-1929)
Park Street, Boston, 1909
Oil on canvas
16 x 20 inches (40.6 x 50.8 cm)
Signed and dated lower left: *A.C. Goodwin / '09*

PROPERTY FROM A NEW YORK ESTATE

PROVENANCE:
Christie's East, New York, *American Paintings and Sculpture*, October 1, 1998, lot 128;
Private collector, New York, acquired from the above;
By bequest to the present owner.

Estimate: $6,000-$8,000

64119

CHAUNCEY FOSTER RYDER
(American, 1868-1949)
Winter Landscape with Pond
Oil on panel
10-3/8 x 13-3/4 inches (26.4 x 34.9 cm)
Signed lower left: *C.F. Ryder*

Estimate: $1,000-$1,500

64120

ROBERT WILLIAM WOOD (American, 1889-1979)
Winter Landscape
Oil on canvas
25 x 30 inches (63.5 x 76.2 cm)
Signed lower right: *Robt. Wood*

Estimate: $6,000-$9,000

64121

BIRGER SANDZÉN (American, 1871-1954)
In the Canyon (North Saint Vrain, Colorado), 1942
Oil on panel
25 x 30 inches (63.5 x 76.2 cm)
Signed lower right: *Birger Sandzén*
Signed, dated, and inscribed indistinctly verso: *In the Canyon / (North Saint Vrain, Colo) / 1942 / Birger Sandzen / Lindsborg, Kansas / Presented to / Rachael Jane / 1973 / L.S. Cougdon* (?)

PROVENANCE:
The artist;
Private collector, acquired from the above, 1942;
Private collector, Dallas, by descent from the above.

NOTE:
This painting retains its original frame, carved by the artist.

We wish to thank Kyle MacMillan for granting permission to reprint below his article "New Appreciation for Birger Sandzén's Singular Colorado Landscapes," originally published in *The Denver Post*, October 1, 2011:

No painter ever has captured the Colorado landscape with more vibrant colors and livelier brushwork than Birger Sandzén, and the art world is finally catching on.

For several decades after his death in 1954, the Swedish émigré's Post-Impressionist paintings did not receive the acclaim they deserved, in part because he spent his entire career far from the all-important New York scene. . . . [A]ll that has changed in recent years, as an increasing number of collectors and museums scramble to acquire one of the 2,800 or so paintings he produced in his lifetime, and prices for his works continue to escalate.

"I have been in many places, but there is none which adapts itself any more to my desires than this," Sandzén said of the Pikes Peak region in 1923.

Rooted in Post-Impressionism, Sandzén's mature style combines vibrant, often non-objective colors, with thick, energetic applications of paint, with which the artist almost sculpturally suggests the craggy contours of rocks and canyons. But Sandzén was no stickler for representational accuracy. He had no qualms about substituting backgrounds or making other modifications to a scene to achieve the kind of balanced composition he was seeking.

In 1894, the artist spent six months studying in the Parisian studio of Edmond-Francois Aman-Jean, a colleague of Georges Seurat. That time in Paris, then the epicenter of the art world, transformed Sandzén and put him on the road toward a distinctive Post-Impressionist style that loosely resembles that of certain other painters but is instantly and unmistakably identifiable as his.

Later, he switched to a more muted palette, which can be seen in *In the Canyon (North Saint Vrain, Colorado)*, 1942.

An important dimension of Sandzén's work is his connection to American Fauvism, an important but still underappreciated facet of modernist painting in this country.

Estimate: $70,000-$90,000

64122

MORT KÜNSTLER (American, b. 1931)
Fighting 69th: General Meagher and the Irish Brigade, Fredericksburg, Virginia, December 2, 1862, 1998
Oil on canvas
26 x 48 inches (66.0 x 121.9 cm)
Signed and dated lower right: © MKünstler '98
Titled, signed, and dated on upper stretcher bar verso: *Fighting 69th / General Meagher and the Irish Brigade MKünstler '98*

Estimate: $30,000-$50,000

From portraits of prehistoric American life to the odyssey of the space shuttle, Mort Künstler paints America's story. In the early 1980s, he began focusing mainly on the American Civil War. "Mort Künstler is the foremost Civil War artist of our time-if not of all time," says Dr. James I. Robertson Jr., author of the celebrated biography, *Stonewall Jackson*. "To study his paintings," says Robertson, "is to simply see history alive." Künstler's *Fighting 69th: General Meagher and the Irish Brigade, Fredericksburg, Virginia, December 2, 1862*, painted in 1998, perfectly encapsulates the courage and honor of the 'Fighting Irish' in that infamous battle, and showcases Künstler's virtuosity as the greatest painter of American history alive today.

The Irish Brigade was an infantry brigade, consisting predominantly of Irish Americans that served in the Union Army in the Civil War. The designation of the first regiment in the brigade, the 69th New York Infantry, or the "Fighting 69th," continued in later wars. The Irish Brigade was known in part for its famous war cry, the "faugh a ballagh," which is an Anglicization of the Irish phrase, *fág an bealach*, meaning "clear the way". According to Fox's *Regimental Losses*, of all Union army brigades, only the 1st Vermont Brigade and Iron Brigade suffered more combat dead than the Irish Brigade during the Civil War.

The brigade suffered its most severe casualties at the Battle of Fredericksburg in December 1862, where its fighting force was reduced from over 1600 to 256. Among the countless claims to valor that cold and bloody day would be the reputation earned by the soldiers of the 69th New York. They would charge into the flame of battle at Fredericksburg without their battle flag, which had been shot to ribbons in earlier fighting. Determined to "show the green," the men of the 69th would make their assault with sprigs of boxwood tucked into their kepis. They would indeed "show the green," and in doing so they would also show their pluck and prove their reputation as "The Fighting 69th."

In the present work Künstler paints his soldiers, their tattered green flag flying, poised to face Lee's legions and suffer inimitable loss. Every detail of the scene is meticulously accurate and painstakingly rendered. Kunstler notes:

"I painted *The Fighting 69th* because so many people asked for it. In 1991, I accepted a commission from the U.S. Army War College to paint "Raise the Colors and Follow Me!" It showed General Thomas Francis Meagher and the Irish Brigade charging the Sunken Road at Antietam. For this Irish Brigade picture, I selected a Fredericksburg scene.

"The Federal army arrived on the north side of the Rappahannock River across from Fredericksburg on November 17, 1862. The men believed there would be no more fighting that year and began building winter quarters on November 20th, before official orders were issued to set up winter camp. The army required an enormous amount of wood for shelter and sustenance. Consequently, whole forests disappeared within months, as is seen on the distant hills.

"It snowed on November 29th and since I enjoy painting snow scenes, I knew the picture had to take place sometime after this date. I planned to feature the famous 69th New York but the regiment had no green flag during the battle of Fredericksburg. Tattered and torn from previous fighting, it has been returned to New York to be replaced. Happily, I found that the colors were not retired until December 2nd, so the distinctive and colorful flag would still be present for my painting.

"I contacted Dr. James I. Robertson, Jr., at Virginia Tech for weather conditions and learned there was a clearing and warming trend that day. The color guard and officers of the 69th arrived at the Brigade headquarters of General Meagher for the official return of the colors. Colonel Robert Nugent points out to General Meagher the spot where the long-awaited pontoons, which arrived on November 26th, have been placed. Other well-known members of the 69th are Capt. John H. Donovan (on horseback to the left with the patch over his right eye) and Major James Cavanaugh (the officer on Donovan's immediate left). Capt. Dennis Sullivan is standing at the far right. The man immediately behind him is Rev. William Corby, who was Chaplain of the 88th NY.

"The green regimental flag still exists today, as do the ribbons. The tears and bullet holes are based on the actual flag. An interesting note is that it says 1st regiment on the flag and not the 69th because the 69th NY was the first regiment of the Irish Brigade. The white and red headquarters flag shows it to be the 2nd Brigade, 1st Division, 2nd Corps. according to General Order 102 of the Army of the Potomac of 24th March 1862. The white marker with gold 69th NYSV also still exists."

All of Künstler's artistic devices come together in his engaging and genuine depiction of *Fighting 69th: General Meagher and the Irish Brigade, Fredericksburg, Virginia, December 2*, 1862. His singular ability to encapsulate American history so accurately and with such artistic vigor has earned him the admiration of collectors worldwide. In 1998, the year in which the present work was painted, the Nassau County Museum of Art in New York sponsored a one-man exhibition of Künstler's work entitled *The Civil War—The Paintings of Mort Künstler*. More than 130 paintings, drawings, and sculptures were gathered together from around the nation. The seven-week exhibition attracted more than 30,000 visitors, surpassing the previous attendance record set by a Picasso exhibit. Künstler's following and popularity among scholars, collectors, and museum-goers underscores the artist's firm ranking as a leading illustrator, not only of our generation, but of all time.

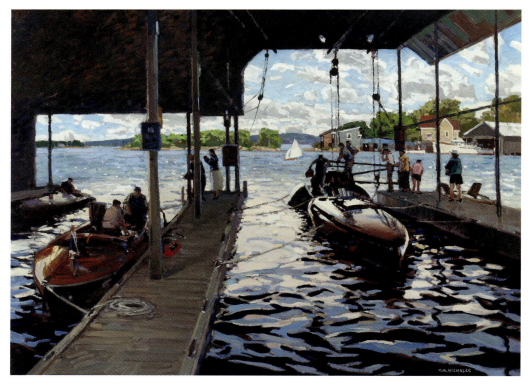

64123

T.M. NICHOLAS (American, b. 1963)
Preparing for the Races, 1996
Oil on canvas
30 x 40 inches (76.2 x 101.6 cm)
Signed lower right: *T.M. Nicholas*
Signed, dated, and inscribed verso: *"Preparing for the Races 1000 Islands/ Clayton Ny. (Antique Boat Museum) No 2 of Boat Museum Series / "Aug. 1996" T.M.N. / "For the Collection of Bob Slack, Not For Sale" T.M. Nicholas*

PROVENANCE:
The artist;
Collection of Robert Slack, acquired from the above;

Private collection, Texas.

Estimate: $5,000-$7,000

64124

T.M. NICHOLAS (American, b. 1963)
Main Street, Nantucket, 1997
Oil on canvas
30 x 40 inches (76.2 x 101.6 cm)
Signed lower right: *T.M. Nicholas*
Signed, dated, and inscribed verso: *"Main Street Nantucket" No. 2 of "Township Series" Nantucket MA. "Idyllic Summer" / "For the Collection of Bob Slack N.F.S." June 97*

PROVENANCE:
The artist;
Collection of Robert Slack, acquired from the above;
Private collection, Texas.

Estimate: $4,000-$6,000

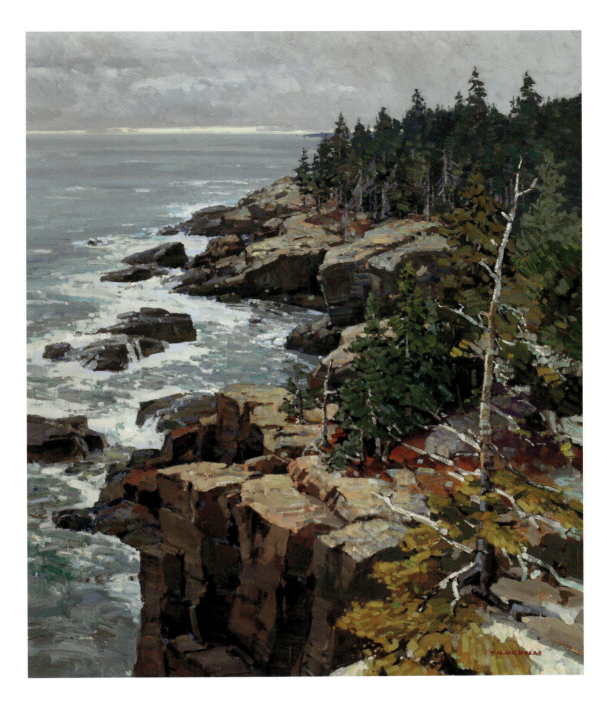

64125

T.M. NICHOLAS (American, b. 1963)
Acadia Cliffs, 1996
Oil on canvas
36 x 30 inches (91.4 x 76.2 cm)
Signed lower right: *T.M. Nicholas*
Signed, dated, and inscribed verso: *T.M. Nicholas Acadia, ME. Feb. 96 / For the Bob Slack Collection N.F.S T.M. Nicholas*

PROVENANCE:
The artist;
Collection of Robert Slack, acquired from the above;
Private collection, Texas.

EXHIBITED:
Rockport Art Association, Rockport, Maine, "First Summer Exhibition," 1996 (labels verso).

Estimate: $10,000-$15,000

64126

STEPHEN SCOTT YOUNG (American, b. 1957)
Sketching, 2004
Watercolor and drybrush on paper
20-3/4 x 22 inches (52.7 x 55.9 cm) (sight)
Signed lower left: *S.S. Young*

PROVENANCE:
John H. Surovek Gallery, Palm Beach, Florida (label verso);
Private collection, Chicago, Illinois, acquired from the above.

Estimate: $50,000-$70,000

64127

STEPHEN SCOTT YOUNG (American, b. 1957)
Yellow Allamanda, 2010
Drybrush and watercolor on paper
11-3/8 x 13-5/8 inches (28.9 x 34.6 cm) (sight)
Signed in pencil upper left: *S.S. Young*
Inscribed in pencil upper right: *Yellow Allamanda*

PROVENANCE:
[With]Adelson Galleries, New York (label verso).

EXHIBITED:
Greenville County Museum of Art, Greenville, South Carolina, "Stephen Scott Young: I'll Be Your Witness," August 8-September 30, 2012 (label verso).

Estimate: $30,000-$50,000

64128

JOHN STOBART (American, b. 1929)
Ship N.B. Palmer Off Golden Gate, 1968
Oil on canvas
36 x 26 inches (91.4 x 66.0 cm)
Signed and dated lower right: *Stobart / © 1968*

PROVENANCE:
Kennedy Galleries, Inc., New York;
Private collection, Dallas;
By descent to the present owner.

Estimate: $10,000-$15,000

64129

JOHN WHORF
(American, 1903-1959)
Barbados
Watercolor, gouache and pencil on paper
21-1/2 x 29-1/4 inches (54.6 x 74.3 cm)
Inscribed in pencil and signed lower left: *To [Vivienne Whorf] / John Whorf*; signed in pencil upper right: *John Whorf*
Inscribed verso: *Barbados*

EXHIBITED:
Adelson Galleries, New York, "American Impressionism and Realism," May 2-July 28, 2011, no. 53.

Hailed as Boston's leading watercolorist, John Whorf was given annual solo exhibitions at the Grace Horne Gallery for much of his career. At least one of Whorf's exhibitions at Grace Horne focused on paintings and watercolors he painted in the West Indies, possibly including the present work.

Estimate: $15,000-$20,000

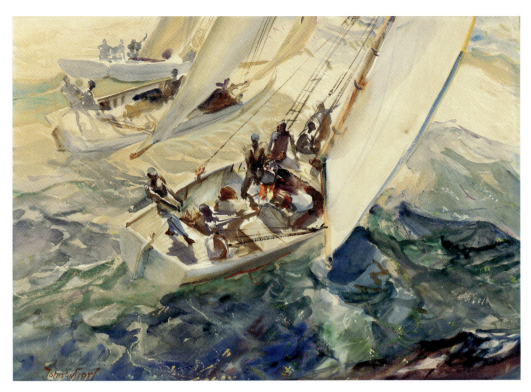

64130

ALBERT E. BACKUS (American, 1906-1991)
Afternoon Florida Landscape, 1985
Oil on canvas
20 x 24 inches (50.8 x 61.0 cm)
Signed and dated lower right: *A.E. Backus 1985*

Estimate: $8,000-$12,000

64131

JULIUS MOESSEL (American, 1872-1960)
A Unique Menagerie
Oil on canvas
29 x 33 inches (73.7 x 83.8 cm)
Signed lower right: *Moessel*
Inscribed verso: *Jul. Moessel /1345 Madison Park / Chicago IL*

PROVENANCE:
Hirschl & Adler Galleries, Inc., New York (label verso).

Estimate: $5,000-$7,000

64132

DONALD ROLLER WILSON (American, b. 1938)
Little Miss Rockwell and Mr. Pooh, 1974
Oil on canvas
48-3/4 x 41-3/4 inches (123.8 x 106.0 cm)
Signed, dated, and inscribed lower right: *LITTLE MISS ROCKWELL AND MR. POOH / DONALD ROLLER WILSON MAY 22, 1972*

Estimate: $6,000-$8,000

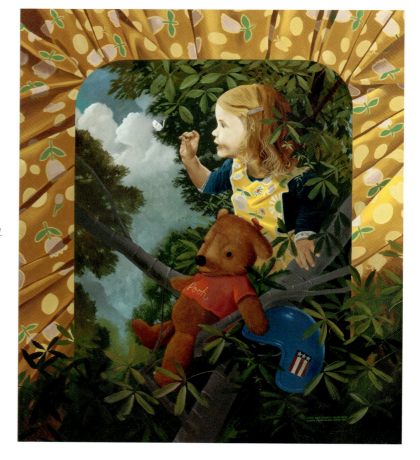

64133

ORVILLE BULMAN (American, 1904-1978)
Madame LaFarge et ses Animal Sauvage, 1975
Oil on canvas
36 x 40 inches (91.4 x 101.6 cm)
Signed lower right: *Bulman*
Inscribed verso: *"MADAME LAFARGE" / ORVILLE BULMAN 1975*

PROVENANCE:
Hammer Galleries, New York (stamp verso).

Estimate: $15,000-$20,000

64134

ORVILLE BULMAN (American, 1904-1978)
Suivez le Premier, 1975
Oil on canvas
16 x 30 inches (40.6 x 76.2 cm)
Signed lower left: *Bulman*
Inscribed, signed, dated verso: *"Suivez le Premier" / Orville Bulman 1975*

PROVENANCE:
Hammer Galleries, New York, 1975 (label verso).

Estimate: $5,000-$7,000

64135

FLETCHER MARTIN (American, 1904-1979)
Seated Girl with Flowers, 1959
Oil on canvas
20 x 28 inches (50.8 x 71.1 cm)
Signed and dated upper right: *Fletcher Martin 59*

Estimate: $4,000-$6,000

64136

BENNY ANDREWS (American, 1930-2006)
Two Figures
Oil and collage with paper and fabric on paper
35-1/2 x 24-1/2 inches (90.2 x 62.2 cm) (sheet)

PROVENANCE:
The artist;
Private collection, acquired from the above;
By descent to the present owner.

Estimate: $3,000-$5,000

64137

EDMUND QUINCY (American, 1903-1997)
After Dinner
Oil on canvas
24 x 29 inches (61.0 x 73.7 cm)
Signed lower right: *Quincy*

Estimate: $800-$1,200

64138

LEROY NEIMAN (American, b. 1926)
Russian Dancers, 1961
Acrylic on board
24 x 31-3/4 inches (61.0 x 80.6 cm)
Signed and dated lower right: *Leroy Neiman 61*

Estimate: $30,000-$50,000

64139
DAVID A. LEFFEL (American, b. 1931)
Friesia, 1994
Oil on artists' board
9-1/2 x 11-1/4 inches (24.1 x 28.6 cm)
Signed with initials and dated lower right: *Daf 94*
Signed, dated, and titled verso

Estimate: $3,000-$5,000

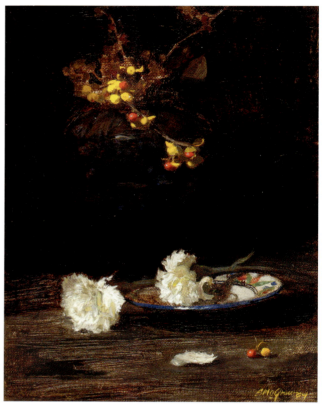

64141
SHERRIE MCGRAW (American, b. 1954)
Carnations and Bittersweet, 1984
Oil on artists' board
11 x 8-3/8 inches (27.9 x 21.3 cm)
Signed and dated lower right: *S McGraw 84*

Estimate: $3,000-$5,000

64140
SHERRIE MCGRAW (American, b. 1954)
Composition for Purple and Green, 1984
Oil on artists' board
8-1/2 x 11 inches (21.6 x 27.9 cm)
Signed and dated lower left: *S. McGraw / 84*

Estimate: $3,000-$5,000

64142

SHERRIE MCGRAW (American, b. 1954)
Bunches of Grapes and a Pear, 1987
Oil on canvas
26-3/8 x 23 inches (66.9 x 58.4 cm)
Signed and dated upper left: *S McGraw 87*

Estimate: $6,000-$8,000

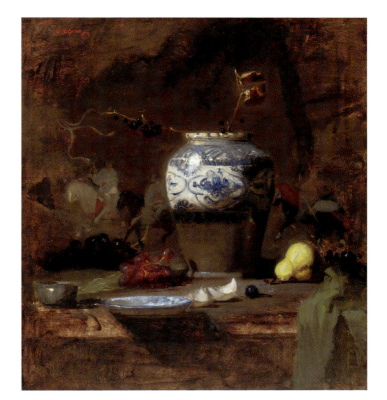

64143

SHERRIE MCGRAW (American, b. 1954)
Pink and White Peonies
Oil on board
8 x 13-3/4 inches (20.3 x 34.9 cm)
Signed upper right: *S McGraw*

Estimate: $3,000-$5,000

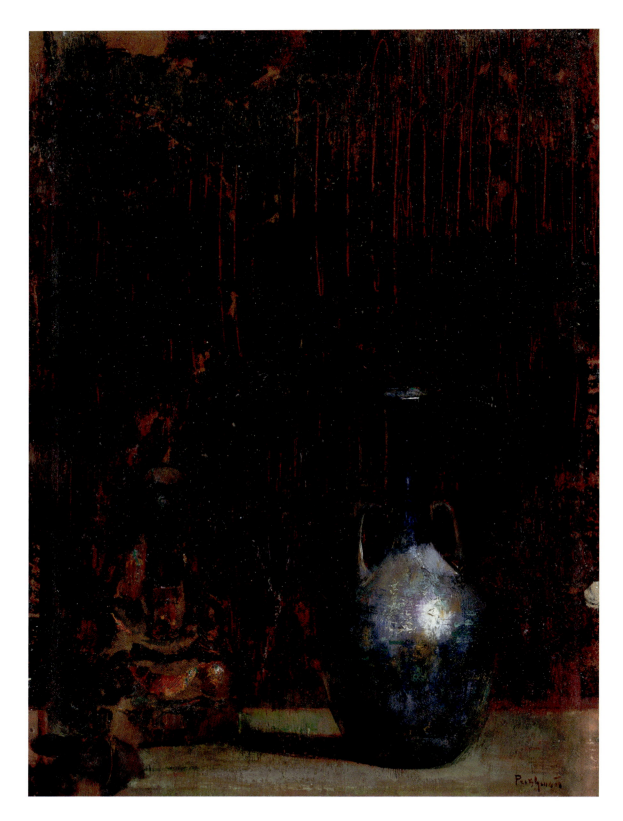

64144

HOVSEP PUSHMAN (American, 1877-1966)
Blue Bottle
Oil on panel
11-1/4 x 8-1/4 inches (28.6 x 21.0 cm)
Signed lower right: *Pushman*

Estimate: $6,000-$8,000

64145

HOVSEP PUSHMAN (American, 1877-1966)
Oriental Still Life
Oil on panel
22 x 14-3/4 inches (55.9 x 37.5 cm)
Signed lower right: *Pushman*

Estimate: $30,000-$50,000

64146

WILLIAM STANLEY HASELTINE (American, 1835-1900)
Venetian Coastline at Sunset, 1872
Oil on canvas
26-1/2 x 51-1/4 inches (67.3 x 130.2 cm)
Signed and dated lower left: *W.S. Haseltine / '72*

PROVENANCE:
Juliet Pierpont Morgan, New York;
Miss Margaret Phair, New York, and Canada, gift from the above;
By descent to the present owner.

William Stanley Haseltine studied art in his hometown of Philadelphia, Pennsylvania and earned his college degree from Harvard University. Following the year of his graduation, Haseltine traveled abroad to Germany to study at the Düsseldorf Academy with a concentration in landscape painting. Over the course of his career, the artist became best known as a landscape and marine painter who had a special talent for conveying light and geological detail, making a prestigious name for himself both in America and abroad. The romantic aesthetic, idealized interpretation of nature and emphasis on tranquility present in Haseltine's landscapes are characteristics associated with the Hudson River School and with Luminism in particular.

Haseltine traveled to countries all over the world in order to paint these sublime scenes and frequently visited Venice. *Venetian Coastline at Sunset* is a prime example of the artist's picturesque compositions where water and sky expand across the entire canvas, creating a sense of romance, serenity and grandness. Pink clouds settle on the horizon along with small, gliding boats and a narrow shore, lined with the buildings of Venice. In the foreground, small sandbars rise up from the water, and isolated wooden posts project a feeling of sweet independence from the busy city. Haseltine pays close attention to detail in the rendering of the ships and gondola, but loosens his brushstrokes as he paints the scene's reflection on the water and the soft, hazy clouds that fill the sky at sunset.

Juliet Pierpont Morgan, sister of Junius Pierpont Morgan (JP Morgan, the financier), gifted *Venetian Coastline at Sunset* to her nurse and companion Miss Margaret Phair, of New York and Canada. It is unclear where or when Mrs. Morgan acquired the work, but the painting has been in the Phair family for at least five decades. It is likely that Venetian Coastline at Sunset has never been offered publicly, until now.

Estimate: $40,000-$60,000

64147

THOMAS SULLY
(American, 1783-1872)
Horace Binney, 1833
Oil on canvas
30 x 25 inches
(76.2 x 63.5 cm)

PROVENANCE:
The artist;
General Thomas Cadwalader, Pennsylvania, acquired from the above;
The Binney family, Pennsylvania;
By descent to the present owner.

LITERATURE:
E. Biddle and M. Fielding, *The Life and Works of Thomas Sully*, Philadelphia, Pennsylvania 1921, p. 102, no. 153.

Horace Binney (January 4, 1780 - August 12, 1875) was an American lawyer who served as an Anti-Jacksonian in the United States House of Representatives.

Born in Philadelphia, Pennsylvania, Binney graduated from Harvard College in 1797, where he founded the Hasty Pudding Club in 1795; he then studied law in the office of Jared Ingersoll, who had been a member of the Constitutional Convention of 1787 and who, from 1791 to 1800 and again from 1811 to 1816, was the Attorney General of Pennsylvania.

Binney was admitted to the bar in Philadelphia in 1800 and practiced there with great success for half a century, and he was recognized as one of the leaders of the bar in the United States. He served in the Pennsylvania legislature between 1806-1807 and was a member of the Whig Party in the United States House of Representatives between 1833-1835. While serving in the House, Binney defended the United States Bank and opposed the policy of President Andrew Jackson.

In *The Life and Works of Thomas Sully*, Edward Biddle and Mantle Fielding describe this portrait of Horace Binney: "Head to left, white stock and high collar to coat. Portrait painted for Genl. Cadwalader, begun Nov. 2nd, 1833, and finished Nov. 15th, 1833. Bust."

Estimate: $7,000-$10,000

64148

ROBERT SALMON (Scottish-American, 1775-1844)
Hagies Rock, Scotland, 1827
Oil on panel
10-1/2 x 15-1/4 inches (26.7 x 38.7 cm)
Signed with initials and dated lower right: *R S 1827*
Partial inscription (appears to be by the artist's hand) and wood block printed labels
verso that read: *Hagies Rock, Scotland / Artist, Salmon*

PROVENANCE:
Kennedy Galleries, Inc., New York (label verso);
Louis J. Dianni, LLC, Fishkill, New York, February 18, 2013, lot 1441.

Estimate: $12,000-$18,000

64149

GEORGE CATLIN (American, 1796-1872)
Ostrich Chase, Buenos Aires, 1857
Oil on canvas
19-1/4 x 27 inches (48.9 x 68.6 cm)
Signed and dated lower left: *G. Catlin 1857*

PROVENANCE:
M. Knoedler & Co., New York, *circa* 1960;
Hirschl & Adler Galleries, Inc., New York;
California Palace of the Legion of Honor, San Francisco, California, loan from the above;
Meredith Long & Co., Houston, Texas;
Mrs. E. Sanders Cushman, Long Island, New York;
Sotheby's, New York, *American Paintings, Drawings and Sculpture*, December 1, 1988, lot 89;
Sotheby's, New York, April 23, 1998, lot 135;
Christie's, New York, *Important American Paintings, Drawings and Sculpture*, May 18, 2004, lot 50;
Private collection, acquired from the above.

LITERATURE:
M.C. Ross, ed., *Episodes from Life: Among the Indians and Last Rambles*, Norman, Oklahoma, 1959, pp. 91-96.

Estimate: $40,000-$60,000

64150

THOMAS MORAN (American, 1837-1926)
A Bit of Acoma, New Mexico, 1911
Oil on canvas
10-1/8 x 12-1/4 inches (25.7 x 31.1 cm)
Inscribed, signed with artist's monogram, and dated lower right: *Acoma / TM 1911*
Bears artist's thumbprint lower left
Titled on label verso

PROVENANCE:
Collection of Mr. and Mrs. Chester R. Colpitt, Tulsa, Oklahoma;
By descent to the granddaughter of the above.

This painting will be included in Stephen L. Good and Phyllis Braff's forthcoming *catalogue raisonné* of the artist's works.

Estimate: $20,000-$30,000

64151

THOMAS MORAN (American, 1837-1926)
Moonrise, Chioggia, Venice, 1897
Oil on panel
19 x 15-1/4 inches (48.3 x 38.7 cm)
Signed with artist's initials in monogram and dated lower left: *TMoran 1897*
Titled on label verso

PROVENANCE:
Wally Findlay Galleries, Inc., Chicago, Illinois;
Collection of Mr. and Mrs. Chester R. Colpitt, Tulsa, Oklahoma (labels verso);
By descent to the granddaughter of the above.

EXHIBITED:
National Academy of Design, New York, November 15 - December 18, 1897.

This painting will be included in Stephen L. Good and Phyllis Braff's forthcoming *catalogue raisonné* of the artist's works.

Regarded as one of the foremost American artists of the nineteenth century, Thomas Moran is best known for his magnificent views of the American West, in particular his detailed depictions of Yellowstone that played a major role in convincing Congress to make the region a national park in 1872. Though the artist spent a great deal of time painting the American frontier, it is his dreamy, jewel-toned depictions of Venice that perhaps best epitomize his intent to imaginatively capture the romantic, picturesque beauty and the unique sensory experience of a locale, rather than depicting reality in topographically accurate detail. As stated by the artist, "All my tendencies are toward idealization. A place as a place has no value in itself for the artist."[1] Indeed, as seen in the present work, Thomas Moran's ability to convey the scenic splendor of the Venice canal in a unique, poetic manner was what would lead to the widespread popularity of his views of the Italian city.

Born in Bolton, England in 1837 as one of seven children, Thomas Moran immigrated to the United States with his family in 1844, settling in Philadelphia. At the age of sixteen, he was apprenticed to a local engraving firm, and spent his spare time painting and drawing. In 1856 the young artist began exhibiting his work at the Pennsylvania Academy of the Fine Arts. Although Moran was self-taught, he received guidance from the painter James Hamilton, who introduced him to the work of the popular English painter Joseph Mallord William Turner. After studying illustrations of Turner's dynamic paintings, Moran was determined to see the artist's work in person. In 1862 he sailed for Britain and spent several weeks at the National Gallery in London studying Turner's works firsthand. Moran began to emulate the artist's atmospheric, light-filled compositions, deriving inspiration from his striking color effects and masterful handling of light, air and mist, as seen in the present work.

Thomas Moran first visited Venice in May of 1886. While there, he produced a number of sketches which he would later develop into oil paintings in his studio. The following spring he exhibited two views of Venice at the National Academy, and thereafter he submitted a Venetian painting to the exhibition nearly every year he participated. The canal was a favorite theme of Moran's, and the subject of Venice quickly became his "best seller." Moran would visit Venice again in 1890, this time returning to New York with a large gondola that he kept on a pond near his summer residence in East Hampton, and which served as a model for many of his Venetian paintings to come.

Works of art and travel literature with Venice as their subject were in abundance and at the height of vogue during the latter part of the nineteenth century, perhaps owing to the exotic, otherworldly concept of a city floating on water. Moran's depictions of the colorful gondolas and fishing boats of Venice fed an American nostalgia for a pre-industrialized past, and served as a counterpoint to a rapidly changing society, which was pressing full speed ahead into a new age.

As exemplified in the present work, Moran, like Turner, took advantage of the mirror-like effects of architecture and fishing vessels reflected on the surface of the water, creating interplay of bright colors and dazzling effects. In *Moonrise, Chioggia, Venice*, a vivid, jewel-toned palette and sweeping brushstrokes enhance the ethereal quality of the scene, transporting the viewer to the idyllic world of Moran's travel recollections.

1: P. & H. Samuels, *The Illustrated Biographical Encyclopedia of Artists of the American West*, 1976, p. 333

Estimate: $60,000-$80,000

64152

JAMES ABBOTT MCNEILL WHISTLER (American, 1834-1903)
Upright Venice (From The Second Venice Set), 1879-80
Etching on paper
10 x 7 inches (25.4 x 17.8 cm)
Ed. IV/VIII
Bears butterfly insignia and the inscription *imp.* in pencil on the tab
Bears notation verso: *W.172. / Upright Venice*

PROVENANCE:
The Vincent Price Collection of Fine Art, Sears, *circa* 1960s;
Private collection, Poulsbo, Washington.

LITERATURE:
E. Kennedy, *The Etched Work of Whistler*, New York, 1910, p. 205.
M. MacDonald, G. Petri, M. Hausberg, and J. Meacock, *James McNeill Whistler: The Etchings, A Catalogue Raisonné*, University of Glasgow, Scotland 2012, online website at http://etchings.arts.gla.ac.uk, G.232.

We wish to thank Professor Margaret MacDonald for her gracious assistance in cataloguing this lot. In Dr. MacDonald's opinion, "the butterfly signature in graphite pencil on the tab is not by Whistler: it is probably by one of his assistants, possibly Mortimer Menpes or Walter Sickert, who helped Whistler to print the Venice etchings."

Estimate: $10,000-$15,000

64153
JOSEPH MORVILLER
(American, 1822-1898)
Wachusett, Massachusetts, from Nature
Oil on canvas
24-1/4 x 36-1/4 inches
(61.6 x 92.1 cm)
Inscribed verso: *Thompson Collection / New York / Geo. P. Rowell*

PROVENANCE:
Collection of Thomas Thompson, Boston, Massachusetts and New York, *circa* 1860s;
Sale: Leeds and Miner, New York, 1870, lot 587;
Private collection, Buffalo, New York.

Estimate: $10,000-$15,000

64154
JAMES DAVID SMILLIE
(American, 1833-1909)
Mountainscape with a Waterfall
Oil on board
8-1/8 x 10-1/8 inches (20.6 x 25.7 cm)
Signed with artist's monogram lower left: *JS*
Inscribed indistinctly verso (possibly the geographical location)

Estimate: $3,000-$5,000

64155

JOSEPH ANTONIO HEKKING (American, 1830-1903)
Canoeing on the Hudson in Autumn
Oil on canvas
20 x 36 inches (50.8 x 91.4 cm)
Signed lower left: *JA Hekking*

PROVENANCE:
Private collection, Cape Cod, Massachusetts.

Estimate: $8,000-$12,000

64156

JOHN WILLIAMSON (American, 1826-1885)
View of the River, 1878
Oil on canvas
12 x 17 inches (30.5 x 43.2 cm)
Initialed and dated lower left: *JW 78*

PROPERTY FROM A NEW YORK ESTATE

PROVENANCE:
Christie's East, New York, *American Paintings & Sculpture*, September 29, 1999, lot 22;
Private collector, New York, acquired from the above;
By bequest to the present owner.

Estimate: $6,000-$8,000

64157

SANFORD ROBINSON GIFFORD (American, 1823-1880)
Lake George from Buck Mountain
Oil on canvas
4-1/2 x 8-1/2 inches (11.4 x 21.6 cm)
The original canvas verso bears the Gifford estate stamp.

PROVENANCE:
Private collection, Texas.

We wish to thank Dr. Ila Weiss for her expertise and gracious assistance in cataloguing this painting. According to Dr. Weiss, in a letter dated July 30, 2013, which accompanies this lot:

This painting bore the Gifford estate sale stamp, verso, before relining, making its identity certain. It is #326 in the *Gifford Memorial Catalogue* (New York: Metropolitan Museum of Art, 1881); and #88 in the estate sale catalogue, *The Sanford R. Gifford Collection, Part II* (New York: Thomas E. Kirby & Co., 1881). . . . The painting was sold in the estate sale of April 29, 1881.

Buck Mountain is a rocky summit on the east side of Lake George with open views to the north and west. A lost larger version of this view was also catalogued, *A View from Buck Mountain, Lake George*, 8 by 18 inches, #325 in the *Memorial Catalogue* and #45 in *The Sanford R. Gifford Collection, Part II*.

In the company of his artist-friends Richard W. Hubbard and Jervis McEntee, Gifford went on a sketching expedition to upstate New York in September 1863, first to Lake Champlain, then to nearby Lake George and on to Lake Placid in the Adirondacks. Gifford had served as a reserve with the Seventh Regiment, New York Militia, in the Civil War that summer for the third and last time, including dangerous active duty during the New York Draft Riots in July. He must have found the subsequent immersion in nature to be especially restorative and delightful.

The trip was documented by Gifford in two sketchbooks, one of them containing Lake George drawings that include the view from Buck Mountain. [Sketchbook 9, New York, 1860-1863, signed "S R Gifford 15 10th St. New York," at the Fogg Museum, Harvard University, ex. coll. Dr. Sanford Gifford.] These drawings are undated but would have been done between September 8, when he dated a view at Lake Champlain and September 17 when they left Bolton on Lake George for the Adirondacks. A panoramic contour drawing of the painting's view extends over two facing pages. Two smaller sketches on a separate page compose the view for a potential painting, and a tiny drawing embedded in one of the compositions tries it with a left foreground. On that page, too, is a tonal drawing of a man seen from behind, standing next to a large rock at the brink of the foreground, with a distance of gray-toned hills and the outline of a far-distant mountain range. He jauntily holds a walking stick to his side to perfectly frame a conifer — an example of the artist's sense of humor. . . . For this character the painting substitutes two figures in the far foreground (as if seen from above), conjured with just a few dabs of paint, undoubtedly representing Hubbard and McEntee. The rock is retained at the edge of the painting's far-foreground, toward the left, as is the string of darker hills in the distance and the far-distant aerial range. Pentimento pencil lines in the painting reveal that a far-foreground hill was tried towards the central area of the lake in the underlying drawing but moved toward the left to balance the composition and conform to the original sketches.

Typical of Gifford's procedure, the small oil sketch transforms the sketchbook's line drawings as a vast aerial-luminous space, conveying the artist's exhilarating experience of the early autumn vista. With sketchy but masterful brushstrokes he establishes the warm tonality of pink-lit cliffs and open slopes of hillside and the warm brown-greens of the foreground's deciduous woods, punctuated with darker evergreens. A scattering of deep salmons and golden highlights among the trees evoke the seasonal coloring. In subtle, cooler opposition are the gray-blues of the hazy distance and upper sky, warming toward tan-pink at the horizon, the warmer and cooler tones mixed in the watery reflection. A middle-distant hilly ridge is sculpted by the warm light and smoothed by intervening air. Still more distant mountains are further flattened in haze, their forms merely suggested where touched by the pinkish light, while the cooler gray far-distance is half-lost in the atmosphere. The lost larger version, in keeping with Gifford's known practice, most likely would have further separated the tangible, substantive foreground from the aerial view through tonal adjustments, and perhaps intensified the autumn color, removing the effect somewhat from that of the original experience captured here.

Gifford was exploring aerial effects, using haze to measure vast expanses, in other works of the early 1860s. Notably similar in composition and effect to the view from Buck Mountain is his *View from Eagle Pond, NJ* of 1862 at the Amon Carter Museum of American Art, Fort Worth. A similar view from a height to the left (which he tentatively tried for the Lake George composition), is a *View of the Berkshire Hills, near Pittsfield, MA* of 1863 at the M. H. de Young Memorial Museum, San Francisco. — *Ila Weiss, July 30, 2013, New York*

Estimate: $8,000-$12,000

64158

GEORGE INNESS (American, 1825-1894)
The Hermit, circa 1883-85
Oil on board
12 x 18 inches (30.5 x 45.7 cm)
Signed lower right: *G. Inness*

PROPERTY FROM A DISTINGUISHED PRIVATE COLLECTOR

PROVENANCE:
Estate of the artist (sold: Fifth Avenue Art Galleries, New York, February 12-14, 1895, no. 21);
Mr. Charles L. Hutchinson, Chicago, Illinois, acquired from the above;
Mr. and Mrs. Carl T. Schuenemann, St. Paul, Minnesota, by descent from the above;
Minnesota Museum of Art, St. Paul, Minnesota, 1966, gift from the above (label verso);
Mr. and Mrs. Myron Kunin, Minneapolis, Minnesota, 1979;
Regis Corporation, Minneapolis, Minnesota;
Christies, New York, December 2, 1988, lot 125 (labels verso);
Collection of Arthur Byron Phillips;
Sotheby's, New York, *American Paintings, Drawings & Sculpture*, December 3, 2009, lot 87;
Acquired by the present owner from the above.

EXHIBITED:
American Fine Arts Society, New York, "Exhibition of the Paintings Left by the Late George Inness," December 27, 1894, no. 189.

LITERATURE:
L. Ireland, *The Works of George Inness: An Illustrated Catalogue Raisonné*, Austin, Texas, 1965, no. 1189, p. 295;
M. Quick, *George Inness: A Catalogue Raisonné*, vol. 2, New Brunswick, New Jersey, 2007, no. 807, p. 136, illustrated.

Estimate: $20,000-$30,000

64159

RICHARD LA BARRE GOODWIN (American, 1840-1910)
Still Life with Game and Hunting Paraphernalia, 1904
Oil on canvas
64 x 36 inches (162.6 x 91.4 cm)
Signed, dated, and inscribed lower left: R LaBarre Goodwin / Copyrighted by / R LaBarre Goodwin / 1904

PROVENANCE:
(Possibly) William Randolph Hearst, California.

Among the foremost American artists to master the high-style *trompe l'oeil* painting that flourished during the late 19th century, Richard La Barre Goodwin is particularly acclaimed for cabin-door scenes like the present work. Populated with hanging game, rifles, gunpowder flasks and other hunting paraphernalia, these canvases were purchased by noted collectors including William Randolph Hearst (to whom the present work is said to have belonged), Senator George Hearst, Governor Leland Stanford and President Theodore Roosevelt, among others.

Estimate: $70,000-$100,000

64160

JAMES BRADE SWORD
(American, 1839-1915)
A Winter's Afternoon, 1874
Oil on canvas
12-1/4 x 20-1/4 inches
(31.1 x 51.4 cm)
Signed and dated lower right:
J.B. Sword 1874

PROPERTY FROM A
NEW YORK ESTATE

PROVENANCE:
Private collection, Belfast, Maine;
Christie's, New York, *American Paintings, Drawings & Sculpture*, March 13, 1996, lot 28;
Private collection, New York, acquired from the above;
By bequest to the present owner.

Estimate: $6,000-$8,000

64161

SAMUEL S. CARR
(American, 1837-1908)
After School
Oil on canvas
12 x 18 inches (30.5 x 45.7 cm)
Signed lower left: *S.S. Carr*

PROPERTY FROM A
NEW YORK ESTATE

PROVENANCE:
John Whalen Fine Art, New York;
Christie's East, New York, *American Paintings & Sculpture*, May 5, 1999, lot 2;
Private collection, New York, acquired from the above;
By bequest to the present owner.

Estimate: $5,000-$7,000

64162

LEVI WELLS PRENTICE
(American, 1851-1935)
Still Life with Apples
Oil on canvas
6-1/2 x 12 inches
(16.5 x 30.5 cm)
Signed lower left:
L.W. Prentice.

PROVENANCE:
Private collection, New York.

Estimate: $8,000-$12,000

64163

HARRY HERMAN ROSELAND
(American, 1866-1950)
Reading the Tea Leaves
Oil on canvas
20 x 24 inches (50.8 x 61.0 cm)
Signed lower right: *Harry Roseland*

Estimate: $4,000-$6,000

64164

EDWARD LAMSON HENRY (American, 1841-1919)
A Country Lawyer, 1895
Oil on canvas
15-1/2 x 22 inches (39.4 x 55.9 cm)
Signed and dated lower left: *EL Henry N.A. 1895*

PROPERTY FROM A NEW YORK ESTATE

PROVENANCE:
Sotheby's, New York, *American Paintings, Drawings & Sculpture*, November 29, 1995, lot 135;
Private collection, New York, acquired from the above;
By bequest to the present owner.

Estimate: $8,000-$12,000

64165

THOMAS BIGELOW CRAIG (American, 1849-1924)
Near the Great Barrington
Oil on canvas board
36 x 60 inches (91.4 x 152.4 cm)
Signed lower left: *Thos. B. Craig*

PROVENANCE:
Berkshire Museum, Pittsfield, Massachusetts;
New Britain Museum of American Art, New Britain, Connecticut;
Hudson River Museum, Yonkers, New York;
Raydon Gallery, New York (label verso).

Estimate: $6,000-$8,000

64166

EDWARD LAMSON HENRY (American, 1841-1919)
Returning from Church, 1864
Oil on paper laid down on canvas
14 x 19 inches (35.6 x 48.3 cm)
Signed and dated lower left: *E.L. Henry 64*
Old label with title verso

PROPERTY FROM A NEW YORK ESTATE

PROVENANCE:
Lore and Rudolf Heinemann;
Christie's, New York, *American Paintings & Sculpture*, October 7, 1997, lot 20;
Private collection, New York, acquired from the above;
By bequest to the present owner.

Estimate: $10,000-$15,000

64167

SAMUEL COLMAN (American, 1832-1920)
Saw Mill Valley, Pennsylvania
Oil on panel
8 x 14-3/4 inches (20.3 x 37.5 cm)
Signed lower left: *Sam Colman*

PROVENANCE:
Private collection, Dallas.

Estimate: $5,000-$7,000

64168

GRANVILLE PERKINS (American, 1830-1895)
Sunday Morning, 1880
Oil on canvas
27 x 22 inches (68.6 x 55.9 cm)
Signed and dated lower left: *Granville Perkins 1880*

PROPERTY FROM A NEW YORK ESTATE

PROVENANCE:
Mrs. George Arden;
Christie's, New York, *American Paintings from the Collection of Mrs. Arden, Part I*, May 22, 1991, lot 67;
Private collector, New York, acquired from the above;
By bequest to the present owner.

Estimate: $4,000-$6,000

64169

JOHN WILLIAMSON (American, 1826-1885)
Running for Shelter, 1860
Oil on canvas
14 x 10 inches (35.6 x 25.4 cm)
Signed with artist's monogram and dated lower left: *JW 60*

Estimate: $3,000-$5,000

64170

HOWARD HELMICK (American, 1845-1907)
The Storyteller, 1885
Oil on canvas
23-1/2 x 32-3/4 inches (59.7 x 83.2 cm)
Signed and dated lower right: *H. Helmick 85*

NOTE:
This painting is housed in a carved Munn frame.

Estimate: $10,000-$15,000

64171

**WILLIAM HENRY LIPPINCOTT
(American, 1849-1920)**
Love's Ambush, 1890
Oil on canvas
28-1/2 x 43-1/2 inches (72.4 x 110.5 cm)
Signed and dated lower left: *Wm. H.
Lippincott / N.Y. 1890.*
Artist's label verso

PROVENANCE:
Galleries Maurice Sternberg,
Chicago, Illinois (label verso).

Estimate: $6,000-$9,000

64172

WILLIAM STANLEY HASELTINE
(American, 1835-1900)
View of the Amalfi Coast, Italy, 1856
Oil on canvas
13-3/4 x 19-3/4 inches (34.9 x 50.2 cm)
Inscribed, signed, and dated verso:
Amalfi by Wm. S. Haseltine 1856

Estimate: $3,000-$5,000

64173

Attributed to ELIHU VEDDER
(American, 1836-1923)
Desolation, circa 1872
Oil on paper laid down on board
7 x 11-7/8 inches (17.8 x 30.2 cm)
Inscriptions verso: *Al. Sig. Federico Zandomeneghi / …Marius 887 / Venezia / disegno/ lucetta / CGL54825-2*
Label verso: *Sketch by Elihu Vedder / for Wm Graham to illustrate / the word "desolation" / 1872 / offered to Mrs. E.B. [Godrell] / Feb. 1894*

PROVENANCE:
The artist;
Mr. William Graham, gift from the above, 1872; (handwritten label verso);
Childs Gallery, Boston, Massachusetts.

Estimate: $2,500-$3,500

64174

**LOUIS ASTON KNIGHT
(American, 1873-1948)**
A Bend in the Stream
Oil on canvas
18-1/4 x 32-1/4 inches
(46.4 x 81.9 cm)
Signed and inscribed lower left: *Aston Knight / Paris*

Estimate: $8,000-$12,000

64175

LOUIS ASTON KNIGHT (American, 1873-1948)
Along the Seine
Oil on canvas
25-1/2 x 32 inches (64.8 x 81.3 cm)
Signed and inscribed lower right: *Aston Knight / Paris*

PROVENANCE:
Rehs Galleries, Inc., New York (label verso).

Estimate: $6,000-$8,000

64176

ROBERT HOPE (British, 1869-1936)
The White Cockade
Oil on canvas
36-1/4 x 28-1/4 inches (92.1 x 71.8 cm)
Signed and dated lower left: *-R. Hope-*

PROVENANCE:
Doig, Wilson & Wheatley, Edinburgh, Scotland (label verso); Christie's, Scotland, *Fine Oil Paintings & Watercolors*, November 26, 1998, lot 737.

Estimate: $8,000-$10,000

64177

CARDUCIUS PLANTAGENET REAM (American, 1837-1917)
Still Life with Flowers on a Table
Oil on canvas
12 x 16 inches (30.5 x 40.6 cm)
Signed lower right: *C.P. Ream*

Estimate: $3,000-$5,000

64182

THOMAS HILL (American, 1829-1908)
Trout Fishing, 1891
Oil on canvas
34 x 27 inches (86.4 x 68.6 cm)
Signed and dated lower right: *T. Hill / 1891*

Estimate: $30,000-$50,000

64183
HERMANN OTTOMAR HERZOG
(American, 1832-1932)
Mountain Lake, Sagne Fjord, Norway
Oil on canvas
14 x 21 inches (35.6 x 53.3 cm)
Signed lower right: *H Herzog*

PROPERTY FROM A NEW YORK ESTATE

PROVENANCE:
Drew Peters Fine Art, Philadelphia, Pennsylvania (label verso);
Christie's East, New York, *American Paintings & Sculpture*, April 9, 1998, lot 63;
Private collection, New York, acquired from the above;
By bequest to the present owner.

Estimate: $4,000-$6,000

64184
EDMUND DARCH LEWIS (American, 1835-1910)
Ships at Sea on a Rocky Coast, 1895
Watercolor, gouache and pencil on board
11 x 21-1/2 inches (27.9 x 54.6 cm)
Signed and dated lower right: *Edmund D. Lewis 1895*

Estimate: $1,200-$1,800

64185
WILLIAM TROST RICHARDS
(American, 1833-1905)
Point Judith, 1871
Watercolor, gouache, and pencil on paper
7-1/2 x 12-3/4 inches (19.1 x 32.5 cm)
Signed and dated lower right: *W.T. Richards 1871*

PROPERTY FROM A NEW YORK ESTATE

PROVENANCE:
Christie's, New York, *American Paintings, Watercolors & Drawings*, September 23, 1992, lot 40;
Sotheby's, New York, *American Paintings, Drawings & Sculpture*, April 23, 1998, lot 39;
Private collection, acquired from the above;
By bequest to the present owner.

Estimate: $3,000-$5,000

64186

ANTONIO NICOLO GASPARO JACOBSEN
(American, 1850-1921)
Three Masted Schooner 'Andrew C. Pierce', 1905
Oil on canvas
30 x 50 inches
(76.2 x 127 cm)
Signed, dated, and inscribed lower right:
ANTONIO JACOBSEN
1905 / 31 PALISADE N.
WEST HOBOKEN NJ.

THE MBNA COLLECTION OF MARITIME ART & SHIP MODELS

Estimate:
$12,000-$18,000

64187

WILLIAM DE LEFTWICH DODGE
(American, 1867-1935)
Surf Under Red Skies,
circa 1906-1920
Oil on canvas
19 x 38 inches (48.3 x 96.5 cm)
Signed lower left: *W. de. Leftwich-Dodge*

PROVENANCE:
Private collection.

EXHIBITED:
Beacon Hill Fine Art, New York, n.d.;
Heckscher Museum of Art, Huntington, New York, n.d.;
Telfair Museum of Art, Savannah, Georgia, "William de Leftwich Dodge: Impressions Home and Abroad," 1998.

William de Leftwich Dodge was a versatile painter who spent his entire career traveling between America and Europe. His *oeuvre* evolved from an academic style in the French Salon tradition to *plein-air* Impressionism, and at the same time grew to encompass a full career as one of America's most successful muralists. By 1921, Dodge was the highest paid muralist in the country, having painted murals for the café at the Hotel Algonquin, New York; the Brooklyn Academy of Music, New York; and for the Court of Jewels at the 1915 Panama-Pacific Exposition in San Francisco. He also taught at Cooper Union in New York from 1916-1929, and at the Art Students League from 1925-1929.

Although Dodge is primarily renowned for his grand-scale murals, his paintings are beautiful examples of American Impressionist paintings. The present work is one of the more atmospheric and intensely colored of Dodge's pictures, painted in Long Island. Dodge often painted the beach of Setauket, but the color and tone of *Surf Under Red Skies* particularly evokes a personal mood.

Estimate: $7,000-$10,000

End of Session Two

Terms and Conditions of Auction

Auctioneer and Auction:

1. This Auction is presented by Heritage Auctions, a d/b/a/ of Heritage Auctioneers & Galleries, Inc., or Heritage Auctions, Inc., or Heritage Numismatic Auctions, Inc., or Heritage Vintage Sports Auctions, Inc., or Currency Auctions of America, Inc., as identified with the applicable licensing information on the title page of the catalog or on the HA.com Internet site (the "Auctioneer"). The Auction is conducted under these Terms and Conditions of Auction and applicable state and local law. Announcements and corrections from the podium and those made through the Terms and Conditions of Auctions appearing on the Internet at HA.com supersede those in the printed catalog.

Buyer's Premium:

2. All bids are subject to a Buyer's Premium which is in addition to the placed successful bid:
- Seventeen and one-half percent (17.5%) on Currency, US Coin, and World & Ancient Coin Auction lots, except for Gallery Auction lots as noted below;
- Nineteen and one-half percent (19.5%) on Comic, Movie Poster, Sports Collectibles, and Gallery Auction (sealed bid auctions of mostly bulk numismatic material) lots;
- Twenty-two percent (22%) on Wine Auction lots;
- For lots in all other categories not listed above, the Buyer's Premium per lot is twenty-five percent (25%) on the first $100,000 (minimum $14), plus twenty percent (20%) of any amount between $100,000 and $1,000,000, plus twelve percent (12%) of any amount over $1,000,000..

Auction Venues:

3. The following Auctions are conducted solely on the Internet: Heritage Weekly Internet Auctions (Coin, Currency, Comics, Rare Books, Jewelry & Watches, Guitars & Musical Instruments, and Vintage Movie Posters); Heritage Monthly Internet Auctions (Sports, World Coins and Rare Wine). Signature® Auctions and Grand Format Auctions accept bids from the Internet, telephone, fax, or mail first, followed by a floor bidding session; HeritageLive! and real- time telephone bidding are available to registered clients during these auctions.

Bidders:

4. Any person participating or registering for the Auction agrees to be bound by and accepts these Terms and Conditions of Auction ("Bidder(s)").
5. All Bidders must meet Auctioneer's qualifications to bid. Any Bidder who is not a client in good standing of the Auctioneer may be disqualified at Auctioneer's sole option and will not be awarded lots. Such determination may be made by Auctioneer in its sole and unlimited discretion, at any time prior to, during, or even after the close of the Auction. Auctioneer reserves the right to exclude any person from the auction.
6. If an entity places a bid, then the person executing the bid on behalf of the entity agrees to personally guarantee payment for any successful bid.

Credit:

7. In order to place bids, Bidders who have not established credit with the Auctioneer must either furnish satisfactory credit information (including two collectibles-related business references) or supply valid credit card information along with a social security number, well in advance of the Auction. Bids placed through our Interactive Internet program will only be accepted from pre-registered Bidders. Bidders who are not members of HA.com or affiliates should preregister at least 48 hours before the start of the first session (exclusive of holidays or weekends) to allow adequate time to contact references. Credit will be granted at the discretion of Auctioneer. Additionally Bidders who have not previously established credit or who wish to bid in excess of their established credit history may be required to provide their social security number or the last four digits thereof so a credit check may be performed prior to Auctioneer's acceptance of a bid. Check writing privileges and immediate delivery of merchandise may also be determined by pre-approval of credit based on a combination of criteria: HA.com history, related industry references, bank verification, a credit bureau report and/or a personal guarantee for a corporate or partnership entity in advance of the auction venue.

Bidding Options:

8. Bids in Signature® Auctions or Grand Format Auctions may be placed as set forth in the printed catalog section entitled "Choose your bidding method." For auctions held solely on the Internet, see the alternatives on HA.com. Review at HA.com/common/howtobid.php.
9. Presentment of Bids: Non-Internet bids (including but not limited to podium, fax, phone and mail bids) are treated similar to floor bids in that they must be on-increment or at a half increment (called a cut bid). Any podium, fax, phone, or mail bids that do not conform to a full or half increment will be rounded up or down to the nearest full or half increment and this revised amount will be considered your high bid.
10. Auctioneer's Execution of Certain Bids. Auctioneer cannot be responsible for your errors in bidding, so carefully check that every bid is entered correctly. When identical mail or FAX bids are submitted, preference is given to the first received. To ensure the greatest accuracy, your written bids should be entered on the standard printed bid sheet and be received at Auctioneer's place of business at least two business days before the Auction start. Auctioneer is not responsible for executing mail bids or FAX bids received on or after the day the first lot is sold, nor Internet bids submitted after the published closing time; nor is Auctioneer responsible for proper execution of bids submitted by telephone, mail, FAX, e-mail, Internet, or in person once the Auction begins. Bids placed electronically via the internet may not be withdrawn until your written request is received and acknowledged by Auctioneer (FAX: 214-443-8425); such requests must state the reason, and may constitute grounds for withdrawal of bidding privileges. Lots won by mail Bidders will not be delivered at the Auction unless prearranged.
11. Caveat as to Bid Increments. Bid increments (over the current bid level) determine the lowest amount you may bid on a particular lot. Bids greater than one increment over the current bid can be any whole dollar amount. It is possible under several circumstances for winning bids to be between increments, sometimes only $1 above the previous increment. Please see: "How can I lose by less than an increment?" on our website. Bids will be accepted in whole dollar amounts only. No "buy" or "unlimited" bids will be accepted.

The following chart governs current bidding increments for Signature auctions; Internet-only auction bidding increments are approximately half of these amounts (see HA.com/c/ref/web-tips.zx#guidelines-increments).

Current Bid	Bid Increment	Current Bid	Bid Increment
< - $10	$1	$10,000 - $19,999	$1,000
$10 - $29	$2	$20,000 - $29,999	$2,000
$30 - $49	$3	$30,000 - $49,999	$2,500
$50 - $99	$5	$50,000 - $99,999	$5,000
$100 - $199	$10	$100,000 - $199,999	$10,000
$200 - $299	$20	$200,000 - $299,999	$20,000
$300 - $499	$25	$300,000 - $499,999	$25,000
$500 - $999	$50	$500,000 - $999,999	$50,000
$1,000 - $1,999	$100	$1,000,000 - $4,999,999	$100,000
$2,000 - $2,999	$200	$5,000,000- $9,999,999	$250,000
$3,000 - $4,999	$250	>$10,000,000	$500,000
$5,000 - $9,999	$500		

12. If Auctioneer calls for a full increment, a bidder may request Auctioneer to accept a bid at half of the increment ("Cut Bid") only once per lot. After offering a Cut Bid, bidders may continue to participate only at full increments. Off-increment bids may be accepted by the Auctioneer at Signature® Auctions and Grand Format Auctions. If the Auctioneer solicits bids other than the expected increment, these bids will not be considered Cut Bids.

Conducting the Auction:

13. Notice of the consignor's liberty to place bids on his lots in the Auction is hereby made in accordance with Article 2 of the Texas Business and Commercial Code. A "Minimum Bid" is an amount below which the lot will not sell. THE CONSIGNOR OF PROPERTY MAY PLACE WRITTEN "Minimum Bids" ON HIS LOTS IN ADVANCE OF THE AUCTION; ON SUCH LOTS, IF THE HAMMER PRICE DOES NOT MEET THE "Minimum Bid", THE CONSIGNOR MAY PAY A REDUCED COMMISSION ON THOSE LOTS. "Minimum Bids" are generally posted online several days prior to the Auction closing. For any successful bid placed by a consignor on his Property on the Auction floor, or by any means during the live session, or after the "Minimum Bid" for an Auction have been posted, we will require the consignor to pay full Buyer's Premium and Seller's Commissions on such lot.
14. The highest qualified Bidder recognized by the Auctioneer shall be the Buyer. In the event of a tie bid, the earliest bid received or recognized wins. In the event of any dispute between any Bidders at an Auction, Auctioneer may at his sole discretion reoffer the lot. Auctioneer's decision and declaration of the winning Bidder shall be final and binding upon all Bidders. Bids properly offered, whether by floor Bidder or other means of bidding, may on occasion be missed or go unrecognized; in such cases, the Auctioneer may declare the recognized bid accepted as the winning bid, regardless of whether a competing bid may have been higher. Auctioneer reserves the right after the hammer fall to accept bids and reopen bidding for bids placed through the Internet or otherwise.
15. Auctioneer reserves the right to refuse to honor any bid or to limit the amount of any bid, in its sole discretion. A bid is considered not made in "Good Faith" when made by an insolvent or irresponsible person, a person under the age of eighteen, or is not supported by satisfactory credit, collectibles references, or otherwise. Regardless of the disclosure of his identity, any bid by a consignor or his agent on a lot consigned by him is deemed to be made in "Good Faith." Any person apparently appearing on the OFAC list is not eligible to bid.
16. Nominal Bids. The Auctioneer in its sole discretion may reject nominal bids, small opening bids, or very nominal advances. If a lot bearing estimates fails to open for 40–60% of the low estimate, the Auctioneer may pass the item or may place a protective bid on behalf of the consignor.
17. Lots bearing bidding estimates shall open at Auctioneer's discretion (approximately 50%-60% of the low estimate). In the event that no bid meets or exceeds that opening amount, the lot shall pass as unsold.
18. All items are to be purchased per lot as numerically indicated and no lots will be broken. Auctioneer reserves the right to withdraw, prior to the close, any lots from the Auction.
19. Auctioneer reserves the right to rescind the sale in the event of nonpayment, breach of a warranty, disputed ownership, auctioneer's clerical error or omission in exercising bids and reserves, or for any other reason and in Auctioneer's sole discretion. In cases of nonpayment, Auctioneer's election to void a sale does not relieve the Bidder from their obligation to pay Auctioneer its fees (seller's and buyer's premium) and any other damages or expenses pertaining to the lot.
20. Auctioneer occasionally experiences Internet and/or Server service outages, and Auctioneer periodically schedules system downtime for maintenance and other purposes, during which Bidders cannot participate or place bids. If such outages occur, we may at our discretion extend bidding for the Auction. Bidders unable to place their Bids through the Internet are directed to contact Client Services at 877-HERITAGE (437-4824).
21. The Auctioneer, its affiliates, or their employees consign items to be sold in the Auction, and may bid on those lots or any other lots. Auctioneer or affiliates expressly reserve the right to modify any such bids at any time prior to the hammer based upon data made known to the Auctioneer or its affiliates. The Auctioneer may extend advances, guarantees, or loans to certain consignors.
22. The Auctioneer has the right to sell certain unsold items after the close of the Auction. Such lots shall be considered sold during the Auction and all these Terms and Conditions shall apply to such sales including but not limited to the Buyer's Premium, return rights, and disclaimers.

Payment:

23. All sales are strictly for cash in United States dollars (including U.S. currency, bank wire, cashier checks, travelers checks, eChecks, and bank money orders, and are subject to all reporting requirements). All deliveries are subject to good funds; funds being received in Auctioneer's account before delivery of the Purchases; and all payments are subject to a clearing period. Auctioneer reserves the right to determine if a check constitutes "good funds": checks drawn on a U.S. bank are subject to a ten business day hold, and thirty days when drawn on an international bank. Clients with pre-arranged credit status may receive immediate credit for payments via eCheck, personal or corporate checks. All others will be subject to a hold of 5 days, or more, for the funds to clear prior to releasing merchandise. (ref. T&C item 7 Credit for additional information.) Payments can be made 24-48 hours post auction from the My Orders page of the HA.com website.
24. Payment is due upon closing of the Auction session, or upon presentment of an invoice. Auctioneer reserves the right to void an invoice if payment in full is not received within 7 days after the close of the Auction. In cases of nonpayment, Auctioneer's election to void a sale does not relieve the Bidder from their obligation to pay Auctioneer its fees (seller's and buyer's premium) on the lot and any other damages pertaining to the lot.
25. Lots delivered to you, or your representative in the States of Texas, California, New York, or other states where the Auction may be held, are subject to all applicable state and local taxes, unless appropriate permits are on file with Auctioneer. (Note: Coins are only subject to sales tax in California on invoices under $1500 and there is no sales tax on coins in Texas) Bidder agrees to pay Auctioneer the actual amount of tax due in the event that sales tax is not properly collected due to: 1) an expired, inaccurate, inappropriate tax certificate or declaration, 2) an incorrect interpretation of the applicable statute, 3) or any other reason. The appropriate form or certificate must be on file at and verified by Auctioneer five days prior to Auction or tax must be paid; only if such form or certificate is received by Auctioneer within 4 days after the Auction can a refund of tax paid be made. Lots from different Auctions may not be aggregated for sales tax purposes..
26. In the event that a Bidder's payment is dishonored upon presentment(s), Bidder shall pay the maximum statutory processing fee set by applicable state law. If you attempt to pay via eCheck and your financial institution denies this transfer from your bank account, or the payment cannot be completed using the selected funding source, you agree to complete payment using your credit card on file.
27. If any Auction invoice submitted by Auctioneer is not paid in full when due, the unpaid balance will bear interest at the highest rate permitted by law from the date of invoice until paid. Any invoice not paid when due will bear a three percent (3%) late fee on the invoice amount or three percent (3%) of any installment that is past due. If the Auctioneer refers any invoice to an attorney for collection, the buyer agrees to pay attorney's fees, court costs, and other collection costs incurred by Auctioneer. If Auctioneer assigns collection to its in-house legal staff, such attorney's time expended on the matter shall be compensated at a rate comparable to the hourly rate of independent attorneys.
28. In the event a successful Bidder fails to pay any amounts due, Auctioneer reserves the right to sell the lot(s) securing the invoice to any underbidders in the Auction that the lot(s) appeared, or at subsequent private or public sale, or relist the lot(s) in a future auction conducted by Auctioneer. A defaulting Bidder agrees to pay for the reasonable costs of resale (including a 10% seller's commission, if consigned to an auction conducted by Auctioneer). The defaulting Bidder is liable to pay any difference between his total original invoice for the lot(s), plus any applicable interest, and the net proceeds for the lot(s) if sold at private sale or the subsequent hammer price of the lot(s) less the 10% seller's commissions, if sold at an Auctioneer's auction.
29. Auctioneer reserves the right to require payment in full in good funds before delivery of the merchandise.
30. Auctioneer shall have a lien against the merchandise purchased by the buyer to secure payment of the Auction invoice. Auctioneer is further granted a lien and the right to retain possession of any other property of the buyer then held by the Auctioneer or its affiliates to secure payment of any Auction invoice or any other amounts due the Auctioneer or affiliates from the buyer. With respect to these lien rights, Auctioneer shall have all the rights of a secured creditor

Terms and Conditions of Auction

under Article 9 of the Texas Uniform Commercial Code, including but not limited to the right of sale. In addition, with respect to payment of the Auction invoice(s), the buyer waives any and all rights of offset he might otherwise have against the Auctioneer and the consignor of the merchandise included on the invoice. If a Bidder owes Auctioneer or its affiliates on any account, Auctioneer and its affiliates shall have the right to offset such unpaid account by any credit balance due Bidder, and it may secure by possessory lien any unpaid amount by any of the Bidder's property in their possession.

31. Title shall not pass to the successful Bidder until all invoices are paid in full. It is the responsibility of the buyer to provide adequate insurance coverage for the items once they have been delivered to a common carrier or third-party shipper.

Delivery; Shipping; and Handling Charges:

32. Buyer is liable for shipping and handling. Please refer to Auctioneer's website www.HA.com/common/shipping.php for the latest charges or call Auctioneer. Auctioneer is unable to combine purchases from other auctions or affiliates into one package for shipping purposes. Lots won will be shipped in a commercially reasonable time after payment in good funds for the merchandise and the shipping fees is received or credit extended, except when third-party shipment occurs. Buyer agrees that Service and Handling charges related to shipping items which are not pre-paid may be charged to the credit card on file with Auctioneer.

33. Successful international Bidders shall provide written shipping instructions, including specified customs declarations, to the Auctioneer for any lots to be delivered outside of the United States. NOTE: Declaration value shall be the item'(s) hammer price together with its buyer's premium and Auctioneer shall use the correct harmonized code for the lot. Domestic Buyers on lots designated for third-party shipment must designate the common carrier, accept risk of loss, and prepay shipping costs.

34. All shipping charges will be borne by the successful Bidder. On all domestic shipments, any risk of loss during shipment will be borne by Heritage until the shipping carrier's confirmation of delivery to the address of record in Auctioneer's file (carrier's confirmation is conclusive to prove delivery to Bidder; if the client has a Signature release on file with the carrier, the package is considered delivered without Signature) or delivery by Heritage to Bidder's selected third-party shipper. On all foreign shipments, any risk of loss during shipment will be borne by the Bidder following Auctioneer's delivery to the Bidder's designated common carrier or third-party shipper.

35. Due to the nature of some items sold, it shall be the responsibility for the successful Bidder to arrange pick-up and shipping through third-parties; as to such items Auctioneer shall have no liability. Failure to pick-up or arrange shipping in a timely fashion (within ten days) shall subject Lots to storage and moving charges, including a $100 administration fee plus $10 daily storage for larger items and $5.00 daily for smaller items (storage fee per item) after 35 days. In the event the Lot is not removed within ninety days, the Lot may be offered for sale to recover any past due storage or moving fees, including a 10% Seller's Commission.

36A. The laws of various countries regulate the import or export of certain plant and animal properties, including (but not limited to) items made of (or including) ivory, whalebone, turtle shell, coral, crocodile, or other wildlife. Transport of such lots may require special licenses for export, import, or both. Bidder is responsible for: 1) obtaining all information on such restricted items for both export and import; 2) obtaining all such licenses and/or permits. Delay or failure to obtain any such license or permit does not relieve the buyer of timely compliance with standard payment terms. For further information, please contact Ron Brackemyre at 800- 872-6467 ext. 1312.

36B. Auctioneer shall not be liable for any loss caused by or resulting from:
   a. Seizure or destruction under quarantine or Customs regulation, or confiscation by order of any Government or public authority, or risks of contraband or illegal transportation of trade, or
   b. Breakage of statuary, marble, glassware, bric-a-brac, porcelains, jewelry, and similar fragile articles

37. Any request for shipping verification for undelivered packages must be made within 30 days of shipment by Auctioneer.

Cataloging, Warranties and Disclaimers:

38. NO WARRANTY, WHETHER EXPRESSED OR IMPLIED, IS MADE WITH RESPECT TO ANY DESCRIPTION CONTAINED IN THIS AUCTION OR ANY SECOND OPINE. Any description of the items or second opine contained in this Auction is for the sole purpose of identifying the items for those Bidders who do not have the opportunity to view the lots prior to bidding, and no description of items has been made part of the basis of the bargain or has created any express warranty that the goods would conform to any description made by Auctioneer. Color variations can be expected in any electronic or printed imaging, and are not grounds for the return of any lot. NOTE: Auctioneer, in specified auction venues, for example, Fine Art, may have express written warranties and you are referred to those specific terms and conditions. .

39. Auctioneer is selling only such right or title to the items being sold as Auctioneer may have by virtue of consignment agreements on the date of auction and disclaims any warranty of title to the Property. Auctioneer disclaims any warranty of merchantability or fitness for any particular purposes. All images, descriptions, sales data, and archival records are the exclusive property of Auctioneer, and may be used by Auctioneer for advertising, promotion, archival records, and any other uses deemed appropriate.

40. Translations of foreign language documents may be provided as a convenience to interested parties. Auctioneer makes no representation as to the accuracy of those translations and will not be held responsible for errors in bidding arising from inaccuracies in translation.

41. Auctioneer disclaims all liability for damages, consequential or otherwise, arising out of or in connection with the sale of any Property by Auctioneer to Bidder. No third party may rely on any benefit of these Terms and Conditions and any rights, if any, established hereunder are personal to the Bidder and may not be assigned. Any statement made by the Auctioneer is an opinion and does not constitute a warranty or representation. No employee of Auctioneer may alter these Terms and Conditions, and, unless signed by a principal of Auctioneer, any such alteration is null and void.

42. Auctioneer shall not be liable for breakage of glass or damage to frames (patent or latent); such defects, in any event, shall not be a basis for any claim for return or reduction in purchase price.

Release:

43. In consideration of participation in the Auction and the placing of a bid, Bidder expressly releases Auctioneer, its officers, directors and employees, its affiliates, and its outside experts that provide second opines, from any and all claims, cause of action, chose of action, whether at law or equity or any arbitration or mediation rights existing under the rules of any professional society or affiliation based upon the assigned description, or a derivative theory, breach of warranty express or implied, representation or other matter set forth within these Terms and Conditions of Auction or otherwise. In the event of a claim, Bidder agrees that such rights and privileges conferred therein are strictly construed as specifically declared herein; e.g., authenticity, typographical error, etc. and are the exclusive remedy. Bidder, by non-compliance to these express terms of a granted remedy, shall waive any claim against Auctioneer.

44. Notice: Some Property sold by Auctioneer are inherently dangerous e.g. firearms, cannons, and small items that may be swallowed or ingested or may have latent defects all of which may cause harm to a person. Purchaser accepts all risk of loss or damage from its purchase of these items and Auctioneer disclaims any liability whether under contract or tort for damages and losses, direct or inconsequential, and expressly disclaims any warranty as to safety or usage of any lot sold.

Dispute Resolution and Arbitration Provision:

45. By placing a bid or otherwise participating in the auction, Bidder accepts these Terms and Conditions of Auction, and specifically agrees to the dispute resolution provided herein. Consumer disputes shall be resolved through court litigation which has an exclusive Dallas, Texas venue clause and jury waiver. Non-consumer dispute shall be determined in binding arbitration which arbitration replaces the right to go to court, including the right to a jury trial.

46. Auctioneer in no event shall be responsible for consequential damages, incidental damages, compensatory damages, or any other damages arising or claimed to be arising from the auction of any lot. In the event that Auctioneer cannot deliver the lot or subsequently it is established that the lot lacks title, or other transfer or condition issue is claimed, in such cases the sole remedy shall be limited to rescission of sale and refund of the amount paid by Bidder; in no case shall Auctioneer's maximum liability exceed the high bid on that lot, which bid shall be deemed for all purposes the value of the lot. After one year has elapsed, Auctioneer's maximum liability shall be limited to any commissions and fees Auctioneer earned on that lot.

47. In the event of an attribution error, Auctioneer may at its sole discretion, correct the error on the Internet, or, if discovered at a later date, to refund the buyer's purchase price without further obligation.

48. Exclusive Dispute Resolution Process: All claims, disputes, or controversies in connection with, relating to and /or arising out of your Participation in the Auction or purchase of any lot, any interpretation of the Terms and Conditions of Sale or any amendments thereto, any description of any lot or condition report, any damage to any lot, any alleged verbal modification of any term of sale or condition report or description and/or any purported settlement whether asserted in contract, tort, under Federal or State statute or regulation or any claim made by you of a lot or your Participation in the auction involving the auction or a specific lot involving a warranty or representation of a consignor or other person or entity including Auctioneer { which claim you consent to be made a party} (collectively, "Claim") shall be exclusively heard by, and the claimant (or respondent as the case may be) and Heritage each consent to the Claim being presented in a confidential binding arbitration before a single arbitrator administrated by and conducted under the rules of, the American Arbitration Association. The locale for all such arbitrations shall be Dallas, Texas. The arbitrator's award may be enforced in any court of competent jurisdiction. If a Claim involves a consumer, exclusive subject matter jurisdiction for the Claim is in the State District Courts of Dallas County, Texas and the consumer consents to subject matter and in personam jurisdiction; further CONSUMER EXPRESSLY WAIVES ANY RIGHT TO TRIAL BY JURY. A consumer may elect arbitration as specified above. Any claim involving the purchase or sale of numismatic or related items may be submitted through binding PNG arbitration. Any Claim must be brought within two (2) years of the alleged breach, default or misrepresentation or the Claim is waived. Exemplary or punitive damages are not permitted and are waived. A Claim is not subject to class certification. Nothing herein shall be construed to extend the time of return or conditions and restrictions for return. This Agreement and any Claim shall be determined and construed under Texas law. The prevailing party (a party that is awarded substantial and material relief on its damage claim based on damages sought vs. awarded or the successful defense of a Claim based on damages sought vs. awarded) may be awarded its reasonable attorneys' fees and costs.

49. No claims of any kind can be considered after the settlements have been made with the consignors. Any dispute after the settlement date is strictly between the Bidder and consignor without involvement or responsibility of the Auctioneer.

50. In consideration of their participation in or application for the Auction, a person or entity (whether the successful Bidder, a Bidder, a purchaser and/or other Auction participant or registrant) agrees that all disputes in any way relating to, arising under, connected with, or incidental to these Terms and Conditions and purchases, or default in payment thereof, shall be arbitrated pursuant to the arbitration provision. In the event that any matter including actions to compel arbitration, construe the agreement, actions in aid or arbitration or otherwise needs to be litigated, such litigation shall be exclusively in the Courts of the State of Texas, in Dallas County, Texas, and if necessary the corresponding appellate courts. For such actions, the successful Bidder, purchaser, or Auction participant also expressly submits himself to the personal jurisdiction of the State of Texas.

51. These Terms & Conditions provide specific remedies for occurrences in the auction and delivery process. Where such remedies are afforded, they shall be interpreted strictly. Bidder agrees that any claim shall utilize such remedies; Bidder making a claim in excess of those remedies provided in these Terms and Conditions agrees that in no case whatsoever shall Auctioneer's maximum liability exceed the high bid on that lot, which bid shall be deemed for all purposes the value of the lot.

Miscellaneous:

52. Agreements between Bidders and consignors to effectuate a non-sale of an item at Auction, inhibit bidding on a consigned item to enter into a private sale agreement for said item, or to utilize the Auctioneer's Auction to obtain sales for non-selling consigned items subsequent to the Auction, are strictly prohibited. If a subsequent sale of a previously consigned item occurs in violation of this provision, Auctioneer reserves the right to charge Bidder the applicable Buyer's Premium and consignor a Seller's Commission as determined for each auction venue and by the terms of the seller's agreement.

53. Acceptance of these Terms and Conditions qualifies Bidder as a client who has consented to be contacted by Heritage in the future. In conformity with "do-not-call" regulations promulgated by the Federal or State regulatory agencies, participation by the Bidder is affirmative consent to being contacted at the phone number shown in his application and this consent shall remain in effect until it is revoked in writing. Heritage may from time to time contact Bidder concerning sale, purchase, and auction opportunities available through Heritage and its affiliates and subsidiaries.

54. Rules of Construction: Auctioneer presents properties in a number of collectible fields, and as such, specific venues have promulgated supplemental Terms and Conditions. Nothing herein shall be construed to waive the general Terms and Conditions of Auction by these additional rules and shall be construed to give force and effect to the rules in their entirety.

State Notices:

Notice as to an Auction in California. Auctioneer has in compliance with Title 2.95 of the California Civil Code as amended October 11, 1993 Sec. 1812.600, posted with the California Secretary of State its bonds for it and its employees, and the auction is being conducted in compliance with Sec. 2338 of the Commercial Code and Sec. 535 of the Penal Code.

Notice as to an Auction in New York City. These Terms and Conditions of Sale are designed to conform to the applicable sections of the New York City Department of Consumer Affairs Rules and Regulations as Amended. This sale is a Public Auction Sale conducted by Heritage Auctioneers & Galleries, Inc. # 41513036. The New York City licensed auctioneers are: Sam Foose, #095260; Kathleen Guzman, #0762165; Nicholas Dawes, #1304724; Ed Beardsley, #1183220; Scott Peterson, #1306933; Andrea Voss, #1320558, who will conduct the Sale on behalf of itself and Heritage Numismatic Auctions, Inc. (for Coins) and Currency Auctions of America, Inc. (for currency). All lots are subject to: the consignor's rights to bid thereon in accord with these Terms and Conditions of Sale, consignor's option to receive advances on their consignments, and Auctioneer, in its sole discretion, may offer limited extended financing to registered bidders, in accord with Auctioneer's internal credit standards. A registered bidder may inquire whether a lot is subject to an advance or a reserve. Auctioneer has made advances to various consignors in this sale. On lots bearing an estimate, the term refers to a value range placed on an item by the Auctioneer in its sole opinion but the final price is determined by the bidders.

Notice as to an Auction in Texas. In compliance with TDLR rule 67.100(c)(1), notice is hereby provided that this auction is covered by a Recovery Fund administered by the Texas Department of Licensing and Regulation, P.O. Box 12157, Austin, Texas 78711 (512) 463-6599. Any complaints may be directed to the same address.

Notice as to an Auction in Ohio: Auction firm and Auctioneer are licensed by the Dept. of Agriculture, and either the licensee is bonded in favor of the state or an aggrieved person may initiate a claim against the auction recovery fund created in Section 4707.25 of the Revised Code as a result of the licensee's actions, whichever is applicable.

Rev.10-15-2013

Terms and Conditions of Auction

Additional Terms & Conditions:
FINE & DECORATIVE ARTS AUCTIONS

FINE AND DECORATIVE ARTS TERM A: LIMITED WARRANTY: Auctioneer warrants authorship, period or culture of each lot sold in this catalog as set out in the **BOLD**-face type heading in the catalog description of the lot, with the following exclusions. This warranty does not apply to:

i. authorship of any paintings, drawings or sculpture created prior to 1870, unless the lot is determined to be a counterfeit which has a value at the date of the claim for rescission which is materially less than the purchase price paid for the lot; or

ii. any catalog description where it was specifically mentioned that there is a conflict of specialist opinion on the authorship of a lot; or

iii. authorship which on the date of sale was in accordance with the then generally accepted opinion of scholars and specialists, despite the subsequent discovery of new information, whether historical or physical, concerning the artist or craftsman, his students, school, workshop or followers; or

iv. the identification of periods or dates of execution which may be proven inaccurate by means of scientific processes not generally accepted for use until after publication of the catalog, or which were unreasonably expensive or impractical to use at the time of publication of the catalog. The term counterfeit is defined as a modern fake or forgery, made less than fifty years ago with the intent to deceive. The authenticity of signatures, monograms, initials or other similar indications of authorship is expressly excluded as a controlling factor in determining whether a work is a counterfeit under the meaning of these Terms and Conditions of Auction.

FINE AND DECORATIVE ARTS TERM B: GLOSSARY OF TERMS: Terms used in this catalog have the following meanings. Please note that all statements in this catalog, excluding those in **BOLD**-face type, regarding authorship, attribution, origin, date, age, provenance and condition are statements of opinion and are not treated as a statement of fact.

1. THOMAS MORAN In our opinion, the work is by the artist.
2. ATTRIBUTED TO THOMAS MORAN
   In our opinion, the work is of the period of the artist which may be whole or in part the work of the artist.
3. STUDIO, (CIRCLE OR WORKSHOP) OF THOMAS MORAN
   In our opinion, the work is of the period and closely relates to his style.
4. SCHOOL OF THOMAS MORAN
   In our opinion, the work is by a pupil or a follower of the artist.
5. MANNER OF THOMAS MORAN
   In our opinion, the work is in the style of the artist and is of a later period.
6. AFTER THOMAS MORAN
   In our opinion, this work is a copy of the artist.
7. ASCRIBED TO THOMAS MORAN
   In our opinion, this work is not by the artist, however, previous scholarship has noted this to be a work by the artist.
8. SIGNED (OR DATED)
   The work has a signature (or date) which is in our opinion is genuine.
9. BEARS SIGNATURE (OR DATE)
   The work has a signature (or date) which in our opinion is not authentic.

FINE AND DECORATIVE ARTS TERM C: PRESENTMENT: The warranty as to authorship is provided for a period of one (1) year from the date of the auction and is only for the benefit of the original purchaser of record and is not transferable.

FINE AND DECORATIVE ARTS TERM D: The Auction is not on approval. Under extremely limited circumstances (e.g. gross cataloging error), not including attributions in **BOLD**-face type, which are addressed in Term F below, a purchaser who did not bid from the floor may request Auctioneer to evaluate voiding a sale; such request must be made in writing detailing the alleged gross error, and submission of the lot to Auctioneer must be pre-approved by Auctioneer. A bidder must notify the appropriate department head (check the inside front cover of the catalog or our website for a listing of department heads) in writing of the purchaser's request within three (3) days of the non-floor bidder's receipt of the lot. Any lot that is to be evaluated for return must be received in our offices within 40 days after Auction. AFTER THAT 40-DAY PERIOD, NO LOT MAY BE RETURNED FOR ANY REASON. Lots returned must be in the same condition as when sold and must include any Certificate of Authenticity. No lots purchased by floor bidders (including those bidders acting as agents for others) may be returned. Late remittance for purchases may be considered just cause to revoke all return privileges.

FINE AND DECORATIVE ARTS TERM E: The catalog descriptions are provided for identification purposes only. Bidders who intend to challenge a **BOLD**-face provision in the description of a lot must notify Auctioneer in writing within forty (40) days of the Auction's conclusion. In the event Auctioneer cannot deliver the lot or subsequently it is established that the lot lacks title or the **BOLD**-face section of description is incorrect, or other transfer or condition issue is claimed, Auctioneer's liability shall be limited to rescission of sale and refund of purchase price. In no case shall Auctioneer's maximum liability exceed the successful bid on that lot, which bid shall be deemed for all purposes the value of the lot. After one year has elapsed from the close of the Auction, Auctioneer's maximum liability shall be limited to any commissions and fees Auctioneer earned on that lot.

FINE AND DECORATIVE ARTS TERM F: Any claim as to authorship, provenance, authenticity, or other matter under the remedies provided in the Fine Arts Terms and Conditions or otherwise must be first transmitted to Auctioneer by credible and definitive evidence within the applicable claim period. Auctioneer, in processing the written claim, may require the Purchaser to obtain the written opinion of two recognized experts in the field who are mutually accepted by Auctioneer and Purchaser. Upon receipt of the two opinions, Auctioneer shall determine whether to rescind the sale. The Purchaser's claim must be presented in accord with the remedies provided herein and is subject to the limitations and restrictions provided (including within the described time limitations). Regardless of Purchaser's submissions there is no assurance after such presentment that Auctioneer will validate the claim. Authentication is not an exact science and contrary opinions may not be recognized by Auctioneer. Even if Auctioneer agrees with the contrary opinion of such authentication and provides a remedy within these Terms and Conditions or otherwise, our liability for reimbursement for bidder's third party opines shall not exceed $500. The right of rescission, return, or any other remedy provided in these Terms and Conditions, or any other applicable law, does not extend to authorship of any lot which at the date of Auction was in accordance with the then generally accepted opinion of scholars and specialists, despite the subsequent discovery of new information, whether historical or physical, concerning the artist, his students, school, workshop or followers. Purchaser by placing a bid expressly waives any claim or damage based on such subsequent information as described herein. It is specifically understood that any refund agreed to by the Auctioneer would be limited to the purchase price.

FINE AND DECORATIVE ARTS TERM G: Provenance and authenticity, excluding attributions in **BOLD**-face type, are guaranteed by neither the consignor nor Auctioneer. While every effort is made to determine provenance and authenticity, it is the responsibility of the Bidder to arrive at their own conclusion prior to bidding.

FINE AND DECORATIVE ARTS TERM H: On the fall of Auctioneer's hammer, Buyers of Fine Arts and Decorative Arts lots assumes full risk and responsibility for lot, including shipment by common carrier or third-party shipper, and must provide their own insurance coverage for shipments.

FINE AND DECORATIVE ARTS TERM I: Auctioneer complies with all Federal and State rules and regulations relating to the purchasing, registration and shipping of firearms. A purchaser is required to provide appropriate documents and the payment of associated fees, if any. Purchaser is responsible for providing a shipping address that is suitable for the receipt of a firearm.

FINE AND DECORATIVE ARTS TERM J: Right of Inspection and Return on Certain Lots. Framed Lots estimated at $1000 or less shall not be unframed for inspection and may not be returned based on condition and are sold "AS IS".

Heritage Auctions strongly encourages in-person inspection of lots by the Bidder. While Heritage is not obligated to provide a condition report of each lot, Bidders may feel free to contact the department for a Condition Report and Heritage will attempt to furnish one, but shall not be liable for failing to do so. Condition is often detailed online, but is not included in our catalogues. The Bidder should review online descriptions as the descriptions supersede catalog descriptions and those condition reports otherwise provided. Statements by Heritage regarding the condition of objects are for guidance only and should not be relied upon as statements of fact, and do not constitute a representation, warranty, or assumption of liability by Heritage. All lots offered regardless of a condition report are sold "AS IS".

For wiring instructions call the Credit department at 877-HERITAGE (437-4824) or e-mail: CreditDept@HA.com

New York State Auctions Only

Notice as to an Auction in New York City. These Terms and Conditions of Sale are designed to conform to the applicable sections of the New York City Department of Consumer Affairs Rules and Regulations as Amended. This sale is a Public Auction Sale conducted by Heritage Auctioneers & Galleries, Inc. # 41513036. The New York City licensed auctioneers are: Sam Foose, #095260; Kathleen Guzman, #0762165; Nicholas Dawes, #1304724; Ed Beardsley, #1183220; Scott Peterson, #1306933; Andrea Voss, #1320558, Michael J. Sadler, # 1304630, who will conduct the Sale on behalf of itself and Heritage Numismatic Auctions, Inc. (for Coins) and Currency Auctions of America, Inc. (for currency). All lots are subject to: the consignor's rights to bid thereon in accord with these Terms and Conditions of Sale, consignor's option to receive advances on their consignments, and Auctioneer, in its sole discretion, may offer limited extended financing to registered bidders, in accord with Auctioneer's internal credit standards. A registered bidder may inquire whether a lot is subject to an advance or a reserve. Auctioneer has made advances to various consignors in this sale. On lots bearing an estimate, the term refers to a value range placed on an item by the Auctioneer in its sole opinion but the final price is determined by the bidders. Rev 11-19-12

How to Ship Your Purchases

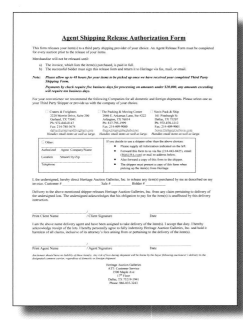

Agent Shipping Release
Authorization form

Heritage Auction Galleries requires "Third Party Shipping" for certain items in this auction not picked up in person by the buyer. It shall be the responsibility of the successful bidder to arrange pick up and shipping through a third party; as to such items auctioneer shall have no liability.

Steps to follow:

1. Select a shipping company from the list below or a company of your choosing which will remain on file and in effect until you advise otherwise in writing.

2. Complete, sign, and return an Agent Shipping Release Authorization form to Heritage (this form will automatically be emailed to you along with your winning bid(s) notice or may be obtained by calling Client Services at 866-835-3243). The completed form may be faxed to 214-409-1425.

3. Heritage Auctions' shipping department will coordinate with the shipping company you have selected to pick up your purchases.

Shippers that Heritage has used are listed below. However, you are not obligated to choose from the following and may provide Heritage with information of your preferred shipper.

Navis Pack & Ship
11009 Shady Trail
Dallas, TX 75229
Ph: 972-870-1212
Fax: 214-409-9001
Navis.Dallas@GoNavis.com

The Packing & Moving Center
2040 E. Arkansas Lane, Ste #222
Arlington, TX 76011
Ph: 817-795-1999
Fax: 214-409-9000
thepackman@sbcglobal.net

Craters & Freighters
2220 Merritt Drive, Suite 200
Garland, TX 75041
Ph: 972-840-8147
Fax: 214-780-5674
dallas@cratersandfreighters.com

- It is the Third Party Shipper's responsibility to pack (or crate) and ship (or freight) your purchase to you. Please make all payment arrangements for shipping with your Shipper of choice.

- Any questions concerning Third Party Shipping can be addressed through our Client Services Department at 1-866-835-3243.

- Successful bidders are advised that pick-up or shipping arrangements should be made within ten (10) days of the auction or they may be subject to storage fees as stated in Heritage's Terms & Conditions of Auction, item 35.

NOTICE of CITES COMPLIANCE; When purchasing items made from protected species.
Any property made of or incorporating endangered or protected species or wildlife may have import and export restrictions established by the Convention on International Trade in Endangered Species of Wild Fauna and Flora (CITES). These items are not available to ship Internationally or in some cases, domestically. By placing a bid the bidder acknowledges that he is aware of the restriction and takes responsibility in obtaining and paying for any license or permits relevant to delivery of the product. Lots containing potentially regulated wildlife material are noted in the description as a convenience to our clients. Heritage Auctions does not accept liability for errors or for failure to mark lots containing protected or regulated species.

rev 3_2013

LUXURY REAL ESTATE AUCTIONS

Feeling pressured to continually lower your list price?

Maybe it's time to move beyond the conventional real estate model to solve your selling dilemma.

Heritage Auctions is now the only top-tier auction house that holds luxury real estate auctions. We offer a powerful platform that reaches a client base of more than 750,000 members worldwide.

Benefits of selling at auction include:

- Your property is guaranteed to be sold within 60-90 days
- High carrying costs such as mortgage payments, insurance, taxes, utilities, HOA dues, membership fees and upkeep will stop
- Selling at auction creates a competitive bidding environment in which fully qualified and motivated buyers participate in a transparent, non-contingent sale

To learn how Heritage Auctions can help you realize the highest attainable selling price for your property listed at $2.5 million or above, email **LuxuryEstates@HA.com** or call **855-261-0573**.

INQUIRIES: 855-261-0573
Scott Foerst | ext. 1521 | ScottF@HA.com
Nate Schar | ext. 1457 | NateS@HA.com
Amelia Barber | ext. 1603 | AmeliaB@HA.com

TX Auctioneer licenses: Samuel Foose 11727; Andrea Voss 16406.
Auction subject to a 10% buyer's premium. See HA.com for details. HERITAGE Reg. U.S. Pat & TM off.

SPORTS COLLECTIBLES AUCTIONS

1927-1928 Lou Gehrig Game Worn New York Yankees Road Jersey.
Realized: $717,000

1965 Mickey Mantle Original Painting by LeRoy Neiman.
Realized: $131,450

1970 Lew Alcindor Game Worn Milwaukee Bucks Jersey.
Realized: $95,600

1909-11 T206 Ty Cobb Bat Off Shoulder PSA NM-MT 8.
Realized: $26,290

1949 Mickey Mantle Signed (Endorsed) New York Yankees Signing Bonus Check.
Realized: $286,800

1910 T206 Eddie Plank SGC 40 VG 3.
Realized: $65,725

Inquiries: 877-HERITAGE (437-4824)
CHRIS IVY | Director, Sports Auctions | CIvy@HA.com | ext. 1319
DEREK GRADY | VP, Sports Auctions | DerekG@HA.com | ext. 1975
ROB ROSEN | VP, Private Sales & Consignments | RRosen@HA.com | ext. 1767
MARK JORDAN | Consignment Director | MarkJ@HA.com | ext. 1187
MIKE GUTIERREZ | Consignment Director | MikeG@HA.com | ext. 1183

Free catalog and *The Collector's Handbook* ($65 value) for new clients. Please submit invoices of $1,000+ in this category, from any source. Include your contact information and mail to Heritage, fax 214.409.1425, email catalogorders@HA.com, or call 866.835.3243. For more details, go to HA.com/FCO.

SEEKING CONSIGNMENTS
DELIVERING RESULTS

THE WORLD'S LARGEST COLLECTIBLES AUCTIONEER
HERITAGE AUCTIONS HA.com

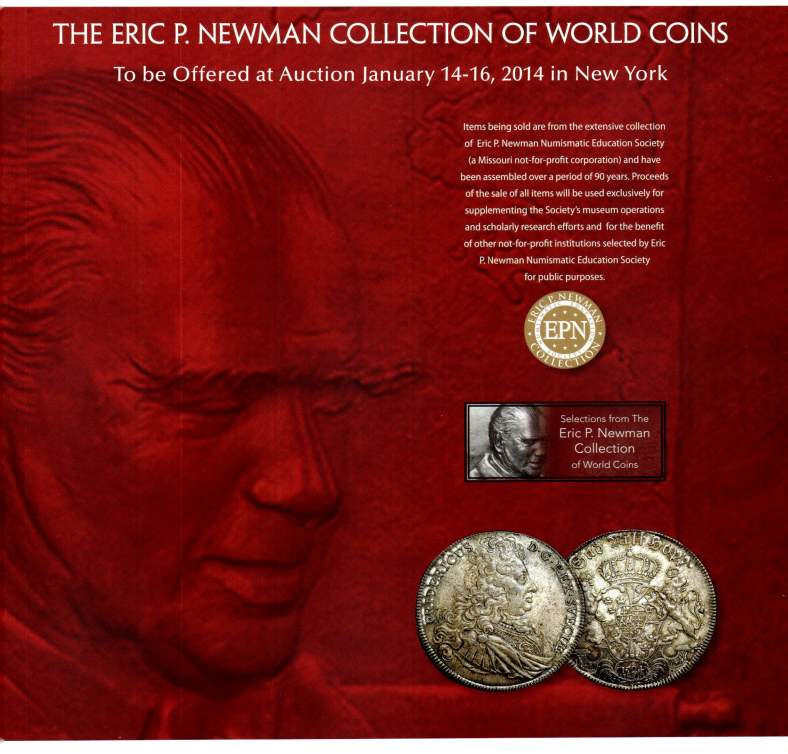

FINE & DECORATIVE ART AUCTIONS

Always Accepting Quality Consignments.
Immediate Cash Advances up to $50 Million.

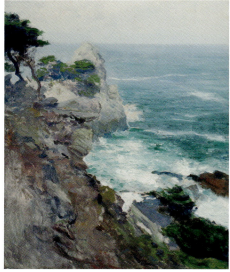

MODERN & CONTEMPORARY ART
FINE PHOTOGRAPHS
November 2

FINE SILVER & VERTU
November 5

EUROPEAN ART
November 8

WESTERN & CALIFORNIA ART
November 14

AMERICAN INDIAN ART
November 15

TEXAS ART
November 16

CONTEMPORARY ART AUCTION:
PROPERTY OF A DISTINGUISHED
GENTLEMAN
November 23

TIFFANY, LALIQUE & ART GLASS
December 4

AMERICAN ART
THE ART OF NEW YORK
December 5

GUY ROSE
Out to Sea, Point Lobos
Oil on canvas. 29.5 x 24 in.
Estimate: $200,000-$300,000
WESTERN & CALIFORNIA ART
AUCTION

HENRI JEAN
GUILLAUME MARTIN
Charmille
Oil on canvas. 32.5 x 31.5 in.
Estimate: $150,000 - $200,000
EUROPEAN ART AUCTION

JASPER JOHNS
0 Through 9, 1970
Lead relief. 30.25 x 23.75 in.
Estimate: $60,000-$80,000
CONTEMPORARY ART
AUCTION: PROPERTY OF A
DISTINGUISHED GENTLEMAN

FREDERICK CARL FRIESEKE
On the Beach (Girl in Blue),
1913
Oil on canvas. 32 x 32 in.
Estimate: $600,000-$800,000
AMERICAN ART AUCTION

Inquiries: 877-HERITAGE (437-4824)

For a free auction catalog in any category, plus a copy of *The Collector's Handbook* (combined value $65),
visit HA.com/CAT29755 or call 866-835-3243 and reference code CAT29755

THE WORLD'S THIRD LARGEST AUCTION HOUSE

PLATINUM® NIGHT & SIGNATURE® AUCTIONS
JANUARY 8-12, 2014 | ORLANDO | LIVE & ONLINE

SELL YOUR COLLECTION ALONGSIDE THESE FUN 2014 HIGHLIGHTS ALREADY CONSIGNED

1913 Liberty Nickel, PR64 NGC, CAC
Second-Finest of Only Five Known
The Olsen Specimen
From The Greensboro Collection

1781 Libertas Americana Silver Medal
Betts-615, EF
From The Marlor Collection

1763 Charlestown Social Club
Betts-508. Bronze. XF-AU
Only Two Held Privately
From The John W. Adams
Collection of Betts Medals

1927-D Twenty Dollar
MS66 NGC
From The Douglas Martin
Collection

1870-S Seated Dollar
Ex: Ostheimer
XF40 PCGS
From The Usibelli Collection

1826 Half Eagle
Extremely Rare BD-2 Die Pair
Ex: Jenks, Newcomer, Akers
MS66 PCGS
From The David & Sharron Akers
Collection

The Finest Known 1795 S-79
Reeded Edge Large Cent
VG10 PCGS; VG8
Ex: Bland; Dr. S.T. Millard; Daniel W. Holmes, Jr.
The First Million Dollar Large Cent
From The Adam Mervis Collection

Consignment Deadline: November 25 | **Inquiries: 800.USCOINS (872.6467)**

Free catalog and *The Collector's Handbook* ($65 value) for new clients. Please submit invoices of $1,000+ in this category, from any source. Include your contact information and mail to Heritage, fax 214.409.1425, email catalogorders@HA.com, or call 866.835.3243. For more details, go to HA.com/FCO.

THE WORLD'S LARGEST NUMISMATIC AUCTIONEER

30318

THE WORLD'S FINEST JEWELRY & HANDBAGS
BY AUCTION AND PRIVATE SALE

Contact Us to Sell Your Pieces Outright or at Auction

Hermès Extraordinary Collection 18cm Diamond Blue Jean Porosus Crocodile Constance with 18K White Gold Hardware
Sold for: $50,000

J.E. Caldwell Art Deco Natural Fancy Blue Diamond, Diamond, Platinum Ring
Sold for: $1,650,500

Van Cleef & Arpels Sapphire, Diamond, Platinum Bracelet
Sold for: $140,500

Hermès 35cm Shiny Blue Electric Porosus Crocodile Birkin
Sold for: $61,250

**Always Accepting Quality Consignments in 38 Categories.
Immediate Cash Advances up to $50 Million.**

Inquiries: 877-HERITAGE (437-4824)

Luxury Accessories
Caitlin Donovan | ext. 3682 | CaitlinD@HA.com

Fine Jewelry
Jill Burgum | ext. 1697 | JillB@HA.com

THE WORLD'S THIRD LARGEST AUCTION HOUSE

For a free auction catalog in any category, plus a copy of *The Collector's Handbook* (combined value $65), visit HA.com/CAT30326 or call 866-835-3243 and reference code CAT30326

QUALIFIED APPRAISALS
BY QUALIFIED APPRAISERS

For Your Fine Art, Jewelry, Wine and Collectibles

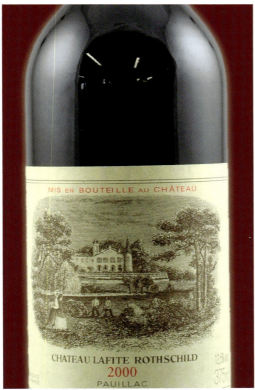

USPAP Compliant Reports for Estates & Insurance

Competitive Rates

Short Turnaround Times

Access to Over 75 Specialists

Confidential Consultations

Inquiries: 877-HERITAGE (437-4824)
Meredith Meuwly, ISA AM
ext. 1631
MeredithM@HA.com

index - The Art of New York

Abbott, Berenice	65016
American School	65017, 65022
Anonymous	65009, 65013, 65018
Asplund, Tore	65023
Ault, George Copeland	65029
Beaton, Cecil (Walter Hardy)	65020
Bodycomb, Rosalyn	65005
Brinkley, Nell	65038
Burckhardt, Rudy	65015
Campbell, Laurence A.	65024
Cornoyer, Paul	65025
Faurer, Louis	65010
Ferriss, Hugh	65003, 65004
Haney, William L.	65001
Henri, Robert	65037
Kanaga, Consuelo	65012
Leibovitz, Annie	65019
Levitz, Jack	65042, 65043, 65044, 65045, 65046, 65047
Nadal, Carlos	65002
Neiman, LeRoy	65039
Pennell, Joseph	65030
Rothbort, Samuel	65034, 65035, 65036
Schwacha, George	65040, 65041
Siebahn, Klaus	65014
Twining, Yvonne	65032
Underhill, Irving	65006
Wiggins, Guy Carleton	65021, 65026, 65027, 65028, 65033
Winter, Ezra	65031

index - American Paintings, Drawings & Sculpture

Andrews, Benny	64136
Audubon, John James	64001, 64002, 64003, 64004, 64005, 64006, 64007, 64008, 64009, 64010, 64011, 64012, 64013, 64014, 64015, 64016, 64017, 64018, 64019, 64020, 64021, 64022, 64023, 64024, 64025, 64027, 64028, 64029, 64030, 64031, 64032, 64033, 64034, 64035, 64036, 64037, 64038, 64039, 64040, 64041, 64042, 64043
Avery, Milton Cark	64095, 64096
Backus, Albert E.	64130
Benton, Thomas Hart	64090, 64091
Betts, Louis	64060
Bewley, Murray Percival	64065
Breckenridge, Hugh Henry	64059
Brown, Anna	64066
Brown, John Appleton	64181
Bulman, Orville	64133, 64134
Burchfield, Charles Ephraim	64094, 64097, 64098, 64099
Butler, Theodore Earl	64053
Carr, Samuel S.	64161
Catlin, George	64149
Cimiotti, Gustave	64102
Coleman, Charles Caryl	64064
Colman, Samuel	64167
Craig, Thomas Bigelow	64165
Crane, Bruce	64097
Cross, Henry Herman	64068
Custis, Eleanor Parke	64062
Dewing, Thomas Wilmer	64178
Dodge, William de Leftwich	64187
Frieseke, Frederick Carl	64054
Frishmuth, Harriet Whitney	64113, 64114
Gifford, Sanford Robinson	64157
Goodwin, Arthur Clifton	64118
Goodwin, Richard La Barre	64159
Gorson, Aaron Harry	64108
Gruppe, Emile Albert	64104
Haseltine, William Stanley	64146, 64172
Hassam, Childe	64051
Hekking, Joseph Antonio	64155
Helmick, Howard	64170
Hennings, Ernest Martin	64052
Henri, Robert	64044
Henry, Edward Lamson	64164, 64166
Herzog, Hermann Ottomar	64183
Hibbard, Aldro Thompson	64117
Hill, Thomas	64182
Hope, Robert	64176
Huntington, Anna Hyatt	64100
Inness, George	64158
Jacobsen, Antonio	64186
Jones, Hugh Bolton	64180
Kalish, Max	64047
Kendall, William Sergeant	64057
Knight, Louis Aston	64174, 64175
Koeniger, Walter	64115
Künstler, Mort	64122
Lachaise, Gaston	64045
Leffel, David A.	64139
Lever, Hayley R.	64107
Lewis, Edmund Darch	64184
Lie, Jonas	64106
Lippincott, William Henry	64171
Lord, Caroline A.	64067
Luks, George Benjamin	64046
Martin, Fletcher	64135
McGraw, Sherrie	64140, 64141, 64142, 64143
Melrose, Andrew	64179
Meyerowitz, William	64088
Moessel, Julius	64131
Moran, Thomas	64150, 64151
Morviller, Joseph	64153
Moses, Grandma	64116
Neiman, LeRoy	64138
Nicholas, T.M.	64123, 64124, 64125
Nichols, Dale	64092
Owen, Robert Emmett	64109
Pearl, Julia	64093
Pène Du Bois, Guy	64048, 64151
Perkins, Granville	64168
Potthast, Edward Henry	64050
Prentice, Levi Wells	64162
Pushman, Hovsep	64144, 64145
Quincy, Edmund	64137
Ream, Carducius Plantagenet	64177
Richards, William Trost	64185
Roseland, Harry Herman	64163
Rumsey, Charles Cary	64069, 64070, 64071, 64072, 64073, 64074, 64075, 64076, 64077, 64078, 64079, 64080, 64081, 64082, 64083, 64084, 64085, 64086
Russell, Morgan	64087
Ryder, Chauncey Foster	64119
Salmon, Robert	64148
Sandzén, Birger	64121
Shinn, Everett	64049
Smillie, James David	64154
Stobart, John	64128
Sully, Thomas	64147
Sword, James Brade	64160
Thieme, Anthony	64111, 64112
Tomanek, Joseph	64105
Vedder, Elihu	64173
Vos, Hubert	64058
Walter, Martha	64061
Waterman, Marcus	64063
Weber, Max	64089
Weir, Julian Alden	64056
Wendel, Theodore	64055
Whistler, James Abbott McNeill	64152
Whorf, John	64129
Wiggins, Guy Carleton	64110
Williamson, John	64156, 64169
Wilson, Donald Roller	64132
Wood, Robert William	64120
Woodbury, Charles Herbert	64103
Young, Stephen Scott	64126, 64127
Zorach, William	64101

Department Specialists

For the extensions below, please dial 877-HERITAGE (437-4824)

Comics & Comic Art
HA.com/Comics

Ed Jaster, Ext. 1288 • EdJ@HA.com
Lon Allen, Ext. 1261 • LonA@HA.com
Steve Borock, Ext. 1337 • SteveB@HA.com
Barry Sandoval, Ext. 1377 • BarryS@HA.com
Todd Hignite, Ext. 1790 • ToddH@HA.com

Animation Art
Jim Lentz, Ext. 1991 • JimL@HA.com

Entertainment & Music Memorabilia
HA.com/Entertainment

Margaret Barrett, Ext. 1912 • MargaretB@HA.com **
John Hickey, Ext. 1264 • JohnH@HA.com
Garry Shrum, Ext. 1585 • GarryS@HA.com

Vintage Guitars & Musical Instruments
HA.com/Guitar

Mike Gutierrez, Ext. 1183 • MikeG@HA.com
Isaiah Evans, Ext. 1201 • IsaiahE@HA.com

Fine Art

American Indian Art
HA.com/AmericanIndian

Delia Sullivan, Ext. 1343 • DeliaS@HA.com

American, Western & European Art
HA.com/FineArt

Ed Jaster, Ext. 1288 • EdJ@HA.com *
Brian Roughton, Ext. 1210 • BrianR@HA.com
Marianne Berardi, Ph.D., Ext. 1506 • MarianneB@HA.com
Ariana Hartsock, Ext. 1283 • ArianaH@HA.com
Kirsty Buchanan, Ext. 1741 • KirstyB@HA.com
Aviva Lehmann, Ext. 1519 • AvivaL@HA.com *

California Art
HA.com/FineArt

Alissa Ford, Ext. 1926 • AlissaF@HA.com ***

Decorative Arts & Design
HA.com/Decorative

Karen Rigdon, Ext. 1723 • KarenR@HA.com
Carolyn Mani, Ext. 1677 • CarolynM@HA.com **

Illustration Art
HA.com/Illustration

Ed Jaster, Ext. 1288 • EdJ@HA.com *
Todd Hignite, Ext. 1790 • ToddH@HA.com

Lalique & Art Glass
HA.com/Design

Nicholas Dawes, Ext. 1605 • NickD@HA.com *

Modern & Contemporary Art
HA.com/Modern

Frank Hettig, Ext. 1157 • FrankH@HA.com
Brandon Kennedy, Ext. 1965 • BrandonK@HA.com

Photographs
HA.com/Photographs

Ed Jaster, Ext. 1288 • EdJ@HA.com
Rachel Peart, Ext. 1625 • RPeart@HA.com

Silver & Vertu
HA.com/Silver

Karen Rigdon, Ext. 1723 • KarenR@HA.com

Texas Art
HA.com/TexasArt

Atlee Phillips, Ext. 1786 • AtleeP@HA.com

Handbags & Luxury Accessories
HA.com/Luxury

Matt Rubinger, Ext. 1419 • Matt@HA.com
Caitlin Donovan, Ext. 1478 • CaitlinD@HA.com

Historical

Americana & Political
HA.com/Historical

Tom Slater, Ext. 1441 • TomS@HA.com
John Hickey, Ext. 1264 • JohnH@HA.com
Michael Riley, Ext. 1467 • MichaelR@HA.com
Don Ackerman, Ext. 1736 • DonA@HA.com

Arms & Armor
HA.com/Arms

Cliff Chappell, Ext. 1887 • CliffordC@HA.com ***
David Carde, Ext. 1881 • DavidC@HA.com ***

Civil War & Militaria
HA.com/CivilWar

David Carde, Ext. 1881 • DavidC@HA.com

Historical Manuscripts
HA.com/Manuscripts

Sandra Palomino, Ext. 1107 • SandraP@HA.com

Rare Books
HA.com/Books

James Gannon, Ext. 1609 • JamesG@HA.com
Joe Fay, Ext. 1544 • JoeF@HA.com

Space Exploration
HA.com/Space

John Hickey, Ext. 1264 • JohnH@HA.com
Michael Riley, Ext. 1467 • MichaelR@HA.com

Texana
HA.com/Historical

Sandra Palomino, Ext. 1107 • SandraP@HA.com

Domain Names & Intellectual Property
HA.com/IP

Aron Meystedt, Ext. 1362 • AronM@HA.com

Jewelry
HA.com/Jewelry

Jill Burgum, Ext. 1697 • JillB@HA.com
Peggy Gottlieb, Ext. 1847 • PGottlieb@HA.com **
Karen Sampieri, Ext. 1542 • KarenS@HA.com *

Luxury Real Estate
HA.com/LuxuryRealEstate

Nate Schar, Ext. 1457 • NateS@HA.com
Scott Foerst, Ext. 1521 • ScottF@HA.com

Movie Posters
HA.com/MoviePosters
- Grey Smith, Ext. 1367 • GreySm@HA.com
- Bruce Carteron, Ext. 1551 • BruceC@HA.com

Nature & Science
HA.com/NatureAndScience
- Jim Walker, Ext. 1869 • JimW@HA.com
- Mary Fong/Walker, Ext. 1870 • MaryW@HA.com
- Craig Kissick, Ext. 1995 • CraigK@HA.com

Numismatics

Coins – United States
HA.com/Coins
- David Mayfield, Ext. 1277 • David@HA.com
- Win Callender, Ext. 1415 • WinC@HA.com
- Chris Dykstra, Ext. 1380 • ChrisD@HA.com
- Mark Feld, Ext. 1321 • MFeld@HA.com
- Sam Foose, Ext. 1227 • Sam@HA.com
- Joel Gabrelow, Ext. 1623 • JoelG@HA.com
- Jason Henrichsen, Ext. 1714 • JasonH@HA.com ***
- Jim Jelinski, Ext. 1257 • JimJ@HA.com
- Jacob Leudecke, Ext. 1888 • JacobL@HA.com
- Bob Marino, Ext. 1374 • BobMarino@HA.com
- Brian Mayfield, Ext. 1668 • BMayfield@HA.com
- James Mayer, Ext. 1818 • JamesM@HA.com **
- Al Pinkall, Ext. 1835 • AlP@HA.com *
- Robert Powell, Ext. 1837 • RobertP@HA.com
- Beau Streicher, Ext. 1645 • BeauS@HA.com

Rare Currency
HA.com/Currency
- Len Glazer, Ext. 1390 • Len@HA.com
- Allen Mincho, Ext. 1327 • Allen@HA.com
- Dustin Johnston, Ext. 1302 • Dustin@HA.com
- David Liu, Ext. 1584 • DavidL@HA.com
- Michael Moczalla, Ext. 1481 • MichaelM@HA.com
- Jason Friedman, Ext. 1582 • JasonF@HA.com

World & Ancient Coins
HA.com/WorldCoins
- Cristiano Bierrenbach, Ext. 1661 • CrisB@HA.com
- Warren Tucker, Ext. 1287 • WTucker@HA.com
- David Michaels, Ext. 1606 • DMichaels@HA.com **
- Matt Orsini, Ext. 1523 • MattO@HA.com
- Sam Spiegel, Ext. 1524 • SamS@HA.com

Sports Collectibles
HA.com/Sports
- Chris Ivy, Ext. 1319 • CIvy@HA.com
- Peter Calderon, Ext. 1789 • PeterC@HA.com
- Tony Giese, Ext. 1997 • TonyG@HA.com
- Derek Grady, Ext. 1975 • DerekG@HA.com
- Mike Gutierrez, Ext. 1183 • MikeG@HA.com
- Lee Iskowitz, Ext. 1601 • LeeI@HA.com *
- Mark Jordan, Ext. 1187 • MarkJ@HA.com
- Chris Nerat, Ext. 1615 • ChrisN@HA.com
- Rob Rosen, Ext. 1767 • RRosen@HA.com
- Jonathan Scheier, Ext. 1314 • JonathanS@HA.com

Timepieces
HA.com/Timepieces
- Jim Wolf, Ext. 1659 • JWolf@HA.com

Wine
HA.com/Wine
- Frank Martell, Ext. 1753 • FrankM@HA.com
- Poppy Davis, Ext. 1559 • PoppyD@HA.com

Services

Appraisal Services
HA.com/Appraisals
Meredith Meuwly, Ext. 1631 • MeredithM@HA.com

Careers
HA.com/Careers

Charity Auctions
Jeri Carroll, Ext. 1873 • JeriC@HA.com

Corporate & Institutional Collections/Ventures
Erica Smith, Ext. 1828 • EricaS@HA.com
Karl Chiao, Ext. 1958 • KarlC@HA.com

Credit Department
Marti Korver, Ext. 1248 • Marti@HA.com

Media & Public Relations
Noah Fleisher, Ext. 1143 • NoahF@HA.com

Museum Services
Erica Denton, Ext. 1828 • EricaS@HA.com

Special Collections
Nicholas Dawes, Ext. 1605 • NickD@HA.com *

Trusts & Estates
HA.com/Estates
Mark Prendergast, Ext. 1632 • MPrendergast@HA.com
Karl Chiao, Ext. 1958 • KarlC@HA.com
Mimi Kapiloff, Ext. 1681 • MimiK@HA.com *
Carolyn Mani, Ext. 1677 • CarolynM@HA.com **

Locations

Dallas (World Headquarters)
214.528.3500 • 877-HERITAGE (437-4824)
3500 Maple Ave. • Dallas, TX 75219

Dallas (Fine & Decorative Arts – Design District Annex)
214.528.3500 • 877-HERITAGE (437-4824)
1518 Slocum St. • Dallas, TX 75207

New York
212.486.3500
445 Park Avenue • New York, NY 10022

Beverly Hills
310.492.8600
9478 W. Olympic Blvd.
Beverly Hills, CA 90212

San Francisco
877-HERITAGE (437-4824)
478 Jackson Street
San Francisco, CA 94111

DALLAS | NEW YORK | SAN FRANCISCO | BEVERLY HILLS | HOUSTON | PARIS | GENEVA

Corporate Officers
R. Steven Ivy, Co-Chairman
James L. Halperin, Co-Chairman
Gregory J. Rohan, President
Paul Minshull, Chief Operating Officer
Todd Imhof, Executive Vice President
Kathleen Guzman, Managing Director-New York

* Primary office location: New York
** Primary office location: Beverly Hills
*** Primary office location: San Francisco

Upcoming Auctions

U.S. Rare Coin Auctions	Location	Auction Dates	Consignment Deadline
U.S. Rare Coins	New York	November 1-2, 2013	Closed
The Eric P. Newman Collection Part II	New York	November 15-16, 2013	Closed
U.S. Rare Coins	Houston	December 5-6, 2013	Closed
U.S. Rare Coins	Orlando	January 8-12, 2014	November 25, 2013

World & Ancient Coin Auctions	Location	Auction Dates	Consignment Deadline
World Coins	New York	January 5-6, 2014	November 8, 2013
The Eric P. Newman World Coin Collection	New York	January 14-15, 2014	Closed

Rare Currency Auctions	Location	Auction Dates	Consignment Deadline
Currency	Orlando	January 8-14, 2014	November 18, 2013
Rare World Paper Money	Orlando	January 8-14, 2014	November 18, 2013

Fine & Decorative Arts Auctions	Location	Auction Dates	Consignment Deadline
Photographs + Modern & Contemporary Art	Dallas	November 2, 2013	Closed
Silver & Vertu	Dallas	November 5, 2013	Closed
European Art + Western & Calif. + American Indian	Dallas	November 8-15, 2013	Closed
Texas Art	Dallas	November 16, 2013	Closed
Modern & Contemporary Art	Dallas	November 23, 2013	Closed
Tiffany, Lalique & Art Glass, Fine American Art, Art of NY	New York	December 4-5, 2013	Closed
The Estate Auction	Dallas	February 22-23, 2014	December 16, 2013
Photographs	New York	April 8, 2014	January 30, 2014
Silver & Vertu	Dallas	May 7, 2014	March 5, 2014
Illustration Art	Beverly Hills	May 8, 2014	February 28, 2014
American Indian + Western & California Art & Texas Art	Dallas	May 16-17, 2014	March 10, 2014
Modern & Contemporary Art	Dallas	May 24, 2014	March 17, 2014
European Art, American Art, Decorative Art	Dallas	June 6-9, 2014	March 31, 2014

Jewelry, Timepieces & Luxury Accessory Auctions	Location	Auction Dates	Consignment Deadline
Timepieces	New York	November 21, 2013	Closed
Fine Jewelry + Luxury Accessories	Dallas	December 9-10, 2013	Closed
Fine Jewelry + Luxury Accessories	New York	April 28-29, 2014	February 25, 2014
Timepieces	Dallas	May 22, 2014	March 21, 2014

Vintage Movie Posters Auctions	Location	Auction Dates	Consignment Deadline
Vintage Movie Posters	Dallas	November 16-17, 2013	Closed
Vintage Movie Posters	Dallas	March 22-23, 2014	January 28, 2014

Comics Auctions	Location	Auction Dates	Consignment Deadline
Animation Art, Comics & Original Comic Art	Beverly Hills	November 20-22, 2013	Closed
Comics & Original Comic Art	Dallas	February 21-22, 2014	January 7, 2014

Entertainment & Music Memorabilia Auctions	Location	Auction Dates	Consignment Deadline
Entertainment & Music Memorabilia	Dallas	December 6, 2013	Closed
Vintage Guitars & Musical Instruments	Dallas	February 14, 2014	December 24, 2013
Entertainment & Music Memorabilia	Dallas	April 12, 2014	February 19, 2014

Historical Grand Format Auctions	Location	Auction Dates	Consignment Deadline
Space Exploration	Dallas	November 1, 2013	Closed
Americana + Legends of the Wild West	Dallas	November 23-24, 2013	Closed
Civil War & Militaria + Arms & Armor	Dallas	December 7-8, 2013	Closed
Historical Manuscripts + Rare Books	Beverly Hills	February 5-6, 2014	December 15, 2013
Texana	Dallas	March 8, 2014	January 15, 2014
Americana & Political & Automobilia	Dallas	March 27, 2014	February 3, 2014
Historical Manuscripts + Rare Books	New York	April 9-10, 2014	February 16, 2014
Space Exploration	Dallas	May 9, 2014	March 18, 2014

Sports Collectibles Auctions	Location	Auction Dates	Consignment Deadline
Sports Collectibles	Dallas	November 7-9, 2013	Closed
Sports Collectibles, Golf	Dallas	December 6-7, 2013	Closed
Sports Collectibles, Platinum Night	New York	February 22-23, 2014	January 3, 2014

Nature & Science Auctions	Location	Auction Dates	Consignment Deadline
Nature & Science + Minerals	Dallas	May 3, 2014	March 7, 2014

Fine & Rare Wine	Location	Auction Dates	Consignment Deadline
Fine & Rare Wine	Beverly Hills	December 13, 2013	November 1, 2013

Domain Names	Location	Auction Dates	Consignment Deadline
Domain Names	New York	November 21, 2013	Closed

HA.com/Consign • Consignment Hotline 877-HERITAGE (437-4824) • All dates and auctions subject to change after press time. Go to HA.com for updates.

HERITAGE INTERNET-ONLY AUCTIONS AT 10PM CT:
- Comics – Sundays
- Movie Posters – Sundays
- Sports – Sundays
- U.S. Coins – Sundays & Tuesdays
- Currency – Tuesdays
- Luxury Accessories – Tuesdays
- Timepiece & Jewelry – Tuesdays
- Modern Coins – Thursdays
- Rare Books & Autographs – Thursdays
- World Coins – Thursdays
- Wine – 2nd Thursdays

Auctioneers: Samuel Foose: TX 11727; CA Bond #RSB2004178; FL AU3244; GA AUNR3029; IL 441001482; NC 8373; OH 2006000048; MA 03015; PA AU005443; TN 6093; WI 2230-052; NYC 0952360; Denver 1021450; Phoenix 07006332. Robert Korver: TX 13754; CA Bond #RSB2004179; FL AU2916; GA AUNR003023; IL 441001421; MA 03014; NC 8363; OH 2006000049; TN 6439; WI 2412-52; Phoenix 07102049; NYC 1096338; Denver 1021446. Teia Baber: TX 16624; CA Bond #RSB2005525. Ed Beardsley: TX Associate 16632; NYC 1183220. Nicholas Dawes: NYC 1304724. Marsha Dixey: TX 16493. Chris Dykstra: TX 16601; FL AU4069; IL 2566-052; TN 6463; IL 441001788; CA #RSB2005738. Jeff Engelken: CA Bond #RSB2004180. Alissa Ford: CA Bond #RSB2005661. NYC 1094963. Kathleen Guzman: NYC 0762165. Stewart Huckaby: TX 16590. Cindy Isennock, participating auctioneer: Baltimore Auctioneer license #AU10. Carolyn Mani: CA Bond #RSB2005661; Bob Merrill: TX 13408; MA 03022; WI 2557-052; FL AU4043; IL 441001683; CA Bond #RSB2004177. Cori Mikeals: TX 16582; CA #RSB2005645. Scott Peterson: TX 13256; NYC 1306933; IL 441001659; IL 2431-052; CA Bond #RSB2005395. Michael J. Sadler: TX 16129; FL AU3795; IL 441001478; MA 03021; TN 6487; WI 2581-052; NYC 1304630; IL 441001421; CA Bond #RSB2005412. Andrea Voss: TX 16406; FL AU4034; MA 03019; WI 2576-052; CA Bond #RSB2004676; NYC #1320558. Jacob Walker: TX 16413; FL AU4031; WI 2567-052; IL 441001677; CA Bond #RSB2005394. (Rev.7-12)